the vikings

KRG Pendlesonn

WINDWARD
NEW YORK LONDON

Designed and produced by
Albany Books
36 Park Street London W1Y 4DE

Copyright © Albany Books 1980

Published in the United States by
Windward Books
575, Lexington Avenue,
New York City 10022.

Originally published in England by
Windward Books, London

Library of Congress Catalog Card No: 79-3247

ISBN 0 8317 9146 2

Printed in Hong Kong

First American Edition

ENDPAPERS: the struggle between
Christianity and the pagan gods, Odin, Thor
and Frey, as symbolized on a twelfth century
Swedish wall-hanging. (*Museum of National
Antiquities, Stockholm; Photoresources*)

TITLE PAGE: Gotland picture stone showing
a scene from Valhalla. (*Michael Holford
Library*)

CONTENTS PAGE: the Viking burial place at
Lindholm Høje in Jutland. Consisting of 628
graves, 200 were marked by the outline of a
ship in stones. (*Werner Forman Archive*)

Contents

Introduction

789 was the year in which the Vikings first spilled blood on English soil. The incident took place at Portland, the great rocky eminence jutting out to sea near the presentday seaside resort of Weymouth. Three ships of Norwegians put in. According to the *Anglo-Saxon Chronicle*, when 'the king's reeve rode there and tried to make them go to the royal manor, for he did not know who or what they were, they slew him. These were the first ships of the Danes to come to England.'

The killing of unfortunate Beaduheard, the official of the Wessex King, only became significant in the minds of people as the initial murderous encounter after Viking raids began in earnest. The real shock of terror was administered by the attack on Lindisfarne four years later. The unexpected savagery of the Viking assault on the renowned monastery shocked men everywhere. From the court of Charlemagne, the York-born Alcuin lamented: 'It is some three hundred and fifty years that we and our forefathers have inhabited this lovely land, and never before in Britain has such terror appeared as this we have now suffered at the hands of the heathen. Nor was it thought possible that such an inroad from the sea could be made. Behold the church of St. Cuthbert spattered with the blood of the priests of God, despoiled of all its ornaments; a place more venerable than all in Britain is given as prey to pagan peoples.' For the year of this traumatic sack the *Anglo-Saxon Chronicle* records that 'terrible portents appeared over Northumbria and sadly frightened the inhabitants; these were exceptional flashes of lightning, and fiery dragons were seen flying in the air . . . [and] a great famine followed soon upon these signs.'

The times were very much out of joint. In Northumbria, Alcuin com-

The ruins of Lindisfarne monastery. This famous foundation of St Cuthbert was destroyed by the Vikings in 793. *(Werner Forman Archive)*

9

mented, 'no-one is free from fear'. It would have been true to say that those settled close to the coast or on the banks of navigable rivers quickly shared this anxiety. The eleventh-century chronicler, Symeon of Durham, tells of raiders over the next few years striking 'like ravening wolves, plundering, devouring and slaughtering'. But the Vikings, he noted with unmonastic glee, did not always get away unscathed. In 794 at Jarrow, south of Lindisfarne, their chief was slain and a storm sank most of their ships, many of the attackers being drowned.

The sudden raids at the end of the eighth century may have startled Christian Europe, but they were little more than harbingers of the Viking onslaught in the ninth century. They did, however, set the tone of the response. Forgetting or overlooking the warlike migrations of their own ancestors in overwhelming and settling the old provinces of the Roman Empire, scholars and clerics like Alcuin castigated the wild Northmen as enemies of civilized living, a curse laid upon sinful men by God. To his contemporaries Alcuin quoted Jeremiah 1:14. 'Then the Lord said unto me, "Out of the north an evil shall break forth upon all the inhabitants of the land".' Yet the ninth-century instrument of wrath was not like the army of Nebuchadnezzar, which had led the Jews away to captivity in Babylon. The 'stinging hornets', as Symeon of Durham termed the Vikings, were not part of a single force, though later on a degree of cooperation arose as colonization replaced raiding as the main objective. The confusing attacks confused the *Anglo-Saxon Chronicle* itself. The record is never quite certain as to whether a particular band or army is Danish or Norwegian. Typically, the account of Beaduheard's death refers to both. It appears that the early raiders were Norwegian, whereas from the 830s onwards they were predominantly Danes.

The Vikings themselves put to sea for a mixture of reasons. Behind every migration are overpopulation and land-shortage, and the archaeological testimony for Scandinavia during the period 750–1050 indicates that these factors operated. In such rude times, too, the distinctions between trade, colonization, piracy, and war were not so finely drawn. A raider could turn trader, or the reverse, as conditions allowed. Nevertheless, this ambiguity

A Viking ship incised on a piece of wood. In swift vessels like these the ferocious raiders of Scandinavia assaulted Christendom in the eigth and ninth centuries. *(Werner Forman Archive)*

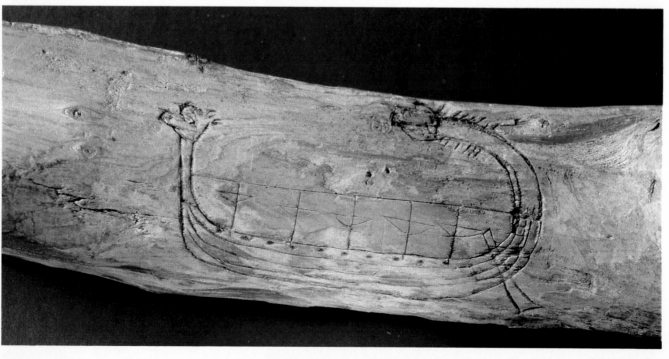

should not obscure the warrior ethic of the Vikings. They revelled in heroic deeds: witness, their daring exploration of the ocean, their delight in battle and contests, their interest in the amazing exploits of the gods.

The Viking homeland of Scandinavia, the Romans believed, was a *vagina nationum*, 'a womb of nations', continually sending forth new waves of migrants. In resisting the Viking wave the Angles, Saxons, and Jutes were simply fighting their more ferocious cousins. Today we call the descendants of the Vikings the Norwegians, Danes, and Swedes. During the period 750–1050 there would have been little sense of nationality. They were all *Nordmanni*, or Northmen, and they transformed themselves into Vikings whenever they set sail in search of trade or plunder. What combined with an undoubted ferocity to create the legendary Viking terror was an extreme mobility. The rivers and seas of Western Europe belonged to the Scandinavian peoples by virtue of their nautical skills. Their dragon-headed longships roamed the flood unopposed.

A Viking. This fierce man was carved on a cart recovered from the Oseberg ship burial, and dates from the ninth century. (*Viking Ships Museum, Bygdoy; Photoresources*)

11

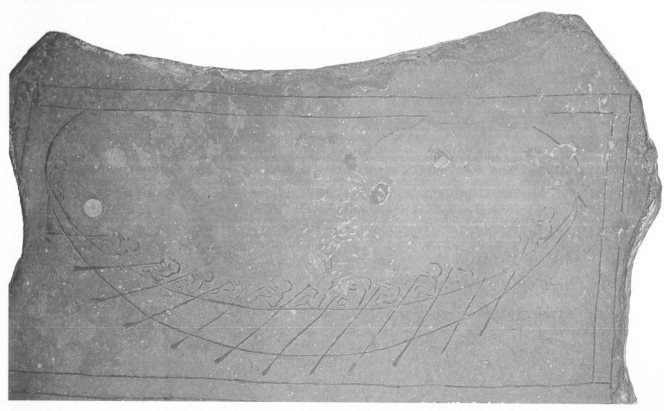

Viking Origins

The earliest inhabitants of Scandinavia were primitive hunters and food-gatherers. Occupation dated from around 10,000 B.C. Later immigrants may have introduced agriculture some time after 3000 B.C., as was the use of metal before 1500 B.C. by the so-called Battle-axe people, who are believed to have been Indo-European. They were certainly fierce warriors. Their art shows four dominant symbols: the sun, the axe, the ship, and the phallus. Boat-shaped graves were favoured, with stones outlining the vessel that would carry the soul of the deceased to the land of death.

About 500 B.C., the beginning of the Iron Age, the climate altered for the worse. Scandinavia became colder and wetter: the winters were sharper, making the difficulties of maintaining livestock during those months more severe. It was during this period of climatic deterioration that the Greek explorer Pytheas reached the area. He set out from Marseilles in the middle of the fourth century B.C. to chart the routes to the tin and amber markets of northern Europe. Six days' sail north of Britain, we are told in later accounts of his voyage, he came to a land situated near the Arctic Circle. He named the country Thule. Its people were poor farmers with few domesticated animals. Diet consisted of wild berries and millet, which had to be threshed in barns on account of the continual rain. Thule was probably the west coast of Norway.

The Romans came into direct contact with Scandinavian people in A.D. 5. Later a Roman fleet sailed as far as the northernmost point of Jutland. From this reconnaissance and subsequent reports the Roman historian Tacitus could at the end of the first century give a reasonable picture of the area. He recorded several peoples and noted their powerful fleets and the unusual style of their vessels which had 'a prow at each end'. Trade between the Roman Empire and Scandinavia was not inconsiderable. Hoards of Roman coins indicate this exchange, but we can be sure that the Scandinavians welcomed earthenware and metal jugs and cups, all kinds of textiles, as well as wine and spices. In return the Romans accepted furs, skins, cattle and slaves, besides amber.

Later historians remarked on the emergence of the *Dani*, the Danes. After the fall of the Roman Empire, the Danes and their Scandinavian neighbours were credited with a ferocious temperament, a strong constitution, and an iron will. The respect accorded to them by the Germanic conquerors of Rome is revealing, for the Goths and the Franks were acknowledging the towering strength of the Northmen in war. As yet this wild energy had not burst on the world in Viking fury.

Legendary tales recall the turbulent rise of the Swedes and the Danes. Tacitus had pointed out the military superiority of the Swedes living in Uppland. Their society was close-knit, so they could move against neighbouring groups as a unit. Their rivals in the sixth and seventh centuries were the Geats, a people

OPPOSITE: a pre-Viking ship, like the craft with 'a prow at each end' mentioned by the Roman historian Tacitus in the first century. (*Museum of National Antiquities, Stockholm; Photoresources*)

This carved animal head once decorated the stern of an early Scandinavian ship. It was found when dredging a Belgian river.
(Photoresources)

living in Gotaland, to the immediate south. Terrible and bloody were the incessant conflicts between the Upplanders and the Geats. Warriors hacked and slashed at each other with great iron swords till one side or the other sought refuge in the fastness of a wood. Many times the battles swung first in favour of the Upplanders, then the Geats. Ongentheow, 'old and terrible', the king of Uppland, died at the hands of the Geat king Hygelac, when the latter's armies stormed his encampment in an unidentified forest. The youngest son of Ongentheow, one Onela, 'best of the sea-kings who gave out treasure in Sweden', wrought a dreadful revenge. But Onela was in his turn killed, as were leaders on both sides until the Geats met their lasting defeat.

The great burial mounds at Old Uppsala are the final resting-places of several of the Swedish kings who died during this period. Excavation has uncovered the charred remains of men of rank and wealth. Inhumation graves ceased from 600 till 900, when cremation was the fashion. Cemeteries in Jutland and Sweden contain both graves with mounds thrown above them and graves surrounded by settings of stones, quite often of large size. The corpse was usually burned in the grave itself and then covered with a layer of earth. At Lindholm Høje in northern Jutland archaeologists excavated a big cemetery in the 1950s. They discovered more than seven hundred graves there, though none of princely status. The usual grave goods were glass beads, small knives, brooches, combs and gaming pieces. After 900, wooden coffins held the dead.

After crushing the Geats, the Swedes extended their power from Uppland into Gotaland as well as onto the island of Gotland. Legend suggests that the Danes, men of the same stock as the Swedes, moved out of Uppland too. According to one tradition it was Dan, son of an Uppsala monarch, who seized the island of Zealand prior to invading Jutland itself. We cannot be certain about the historical truth behind the story. The inhabitants of Jutland, the Danes, acquired a sense of identity somewhat after the Swedes, but the difference in time should not dispose us too much to the legend of Dan. We need to treat with equal care stories concerning later rulers, such as Ro-Hrothgar and Hrolf-Hrothulf. The last-named mounted the throne after a series of bloody feuds and died himself in a revengeful Swedish raid on his stronghold.

Whatever the historical reality behind the heroic struggles of Swedish and Danish war-leaders – and archaeological finds are unlikely to provide us with any personal details – we need to recognize that the homelands of the Swedes and the Danes were then being consolidated. On one hand there was the nucleus of Uppsala, Gotaland, and Gotland; on the other, Zealand, Skane, and Jutland. However, the relation of the Danes to the Angles, Saxons, and Jutes remains obscure. The legendary founder-hero Dan was supposed to have had a brother named Angul, after whom the Angles were known. But the peoples who emigrated from what was to become Denmark may have been on

A seventh century helmet excavated at the Vendel cemetery in Swedish Uppland. Helmets like this fine specimen may have been worn by warriors in the Uppland-Geat wars. *(Statens Historiska Museum, Stockholm; Werner Forman Archive)*

the move before the Danes arose. The relationship was not very distant, though the reaction of Alcuin to the Viking raid of 793 on Lindisfarne precisely demonstrates how the transfer of the Anglo-Saxons to Britain and their incorporation in Christendom had changed them into very different people.

Perhaps the greatest achievement of the pre-Viking era in Scandinavia is the circular stone fort at Eketorp on the island of Oland. This impressively fortified settlement was continuously occupied from 450 to 730, and doubtless, in an emergency, served as a sanctuary for islanders living nearby. Other circular fortresses existed on Oland. The pattern of settlement in the countryside was generally a number of farm buildings, including houses and barns, surrounded by walled fields. Yet hoards of coins should remind us of the recurrent insecurity which lasted well into the eighth century.

The Viking Homeland

Before considering the activities of the Vikings overseas, it is advisable to look at the Viking homeland during the ninth and tenth centuries. By doing so, we shall be able to form a notion of the background from which the daring raiders, traders and settlers sprang, not least because archaeological and historical information is more abundant than in the pre-Viking era.

The three peoples who launched the Viking attacks were the Norwegians, the Swedes, and the Danes. Their own experience in Scandinavia was an apparently endless series of conflicts: wars with each other, or near neighbours; dynastic struggles and family feuds; and folk migration. Danish history can stand as the pattern of the times. Petty kings wrestled for the control of Jutland, Zealand and Skane. Boundaries and alliances were ever changing. Occasionally a ruling house had a run of luck which made it overlord over the majority of the Danes. But permanent control was not maintained by prowess in battle alone, since the resources needed to raise an army derived from agriculture and trade. Only when conditions allowed for greater cohesion in the tenth century do we find the idea of Danish unity firmly established.

The first known use of Denmark was about 950. Gorm the Old, then King of the Danes, had the name inscribed in runes on the memorial stone to his wife Thyri at Jelling. Gorm's successor, his son Harald Bluetooth, left another runic inscription on a stone thirty years afterwards.

His magnificently carved stone has on it the figure of Christ, a great beast locked in struggle with a snake, and the following message: 'King Harald had this memorial made for Gorm his father and Thyri his mother: that Harald who won for himself all Denmark and Norway, and made the Danes Christian'. Harald had certainly remodelled the pagan shrine and cemetery at Jelling; he built a church and, although only his mother had died a Christian, placed his parents' bodies in holy ground. Whether his other claims may be taken at face value is less sure, but they indicate the direction of contemporary Scandinavian affairs.

Christianity and the Roman alphabet took root in Scandinavia during the tenth century. We shall speak of the conversion of the Northmen to Christianity elsewhere. At this juncture a few words on the ancient runic alphabet would not appear out of place. The runes are known for convenience as *futhark*, from the first six letters, rather like our present alphabet is sometimes called the ABC. The letters looked like this:

ᚠᚢᚦᚨᚱ ᚲᚷᚹ:ᚺᚾᛁᛃ
f u th a r k g w h n i j

ᛈᛖᛇᛋ:ᛏᛒ ᛖ ᛗᛚᛜᛟᛞ
p E R s t b e m l ng o d

Two of these manifestly derive from Gothic, namely 'f' and 'th'. Originally twenty-four letters were employed,

17

later only sixteen. The reduction meant that one rune had to serve for more than one sound, causing problems to occur. The runes, signifying literacy, are first found on weapons dating from the third century. An early grave inscription has been discovered in Gotland, but most surviving runic inscriptions are later than the fifth century. As with the development of writing in other parts of the world, runes seemed to the illiterate endowed with mysterious power and authority. Those inscribed on weapons were probably thought to have the efficacy of magic. They acted as a talisman, protecting the person who grasped the weapon. The awe felt by people for the curling runic inscriptions can be gauged in the myths of Odin, the one-eyed god of battle, magic, inspirations, and the dead. It was said that Odin hung himself on Yggdrasill, the cosmic ash, in order to learn the secret runes. A man found preserved in Tollund bog, Jutland, in 1950, may have been hanged on a sacrificial gallows in remembrance of Odin, or a dim predecessor.

The language put down in futhark was Norse, spoken by the Norwegians, the Swedes and the Danes throughout the Viking period. Old Norse bound the Scandinavian peoples together and assisted their overseas expansion by making the speech of the various colonists mutually intelligible. Before 750 the tongue had become differentiated from the Germanic dialects spoken to the south of Scandinavia or in Saxon England. Not until about the year 1000 would dialect differences sharpen sufficiently so as to start the processes by which evolved the modern languages of Norwegian, Swedish, and Danish. Old Norse was therefore the proud tongue of the intrepid searovers. In Iceland, where it was the only form of speech, it has

An eleventh-century runestone from Uppland, Sweden. The stonemason would have cut the letters and the scene beneath with a pointed hammer. *(Statens Historiska Museum, Stockholm; Werner Forman Archive)*

18

descended to the present virtually unaltered.

Apart from a common language, the Scandinavian peoples shared the same social organization, law, art, and religion. Except for the nomadic Lapps inhabiting the tundra, Scandinavia was now a settled agrarian society. The social structure related to the pattern in contemporary Europe. There were three categories of men: the slave, *thrall*; the free peasant, *karl*; and the aristocrat or chieftain, *jarl*. A tenth-century poem, *The Song of Rig*, sheds light on Viking society by telling us how these classes were supposed to have originated. The divinity Rig, the poem says, once approached the mean dwelling of an ancient couple, Ai and Edda, literally Great-grandfather and Great-grandmother. After introducing himself, Rig was given coarse food to quell his hunger and a place in bed between them when it was time to sleep. Rig stayed for three nights and gave them good advice. Nine months afterwards Edda bore a son, Thrall, who was black-haired and ugly, with rough skin, thick fingers, short nails, swollen knuckles, long heels, and a bent back. Thrall took to wife an equally ungainly person, a drudge with crooked legs, dirty feet, sunburned arms, and a big nose. Their multitudinous offspring included boys like Noisy, Roughneck and Horsefly, as well as girls like Lazybones, Beanpole, and Fatty. From these ill-

The preserved Tollund man. He was probably hanged as a sacrifice to Odin, who himself acquired wisdom by hanging on Yggdrasill, the cosmic ash. *(National Museum, Copenhagen; Werner Forman Archive)*

favoured children descended the thralls. Edda's son, Thrall himself, is the archetype of the tiller of the soil, whose anonymous labour sustained untold generations. His back is the image of toil: weighed down by the load he must bear.

Rig visited a second house, warm and better furnished. Inside he encountered an industrious couple, Afi and Amma, literally Grandfather and Grandmother. The well-dressed pair were involved with spinning and weaving: Afi prepared a loom, Amma spun a thread. Once again Rig shared their bed, gave good advice, and departed after three nights. Nine months afterwards Amma bore a son, Karl, who was red and fresh and bright-eyed. Karl took to wife Snor, meaning Daughter-in-law, and their children included boys like Strongbeard, Husbandman, and Smith as well as girls like Prettyface, Maiden and Capable. Together they ran the farms. They were free.

A third dwelling Rig stayed at was a splendid hall belonging to Fadir and Modir, Father and Mother. While Fadir attended to his bow and arrows, Modir attended to her looks and clothes. After a sumptuous meal, accompanied by conversation and drink, Rig slept between his hosts. He dwelt there three nights and gave good advice. Nine months afterwards Modir bore a son, Jarl, who was fair-haired and handsome, with a bright cheek and an eye as piercing as a serpent's. In manhood Jarl could use bow, spear, sword and shield; he could ride and swim and he could hunt excellently.

So it happened that Rig returned to greet Jarl as his special son, for Rig was really the creator of mankind. The divinity gave Jarl his own name, revealed to him the runes, and told him to claim his lands. In obedience to Rig, Jarl rode through the world, fighting and slaying, seizing booty and distributing treasure. At last he married Erna, literally Lively, a fair and wise noblewoman, and she bore

THE VIKING HOMELAND

him twelve sons. One of these remarkable children was Kon, meaning King, who mastered the runes so well he could perform miracles. He was able to cure the sick, prevent storms, and control the forest fire. It was even said that he excelled Rig, being almost a god himself.

This poetic presentation of the Viking social order would seem to be accurate. There was an aristocracy, a body of free man, and a population of slaves. At the very bottom of society, the thrall had no rights: his life was of no account. Usually he would be the descendant of parents captured in a raid, or a border war. The lot of a thrall was hard, yet the slave-owner would have been concerned to keep his slaves, like his cattle, in good condition. The karl, the free peasant, ideally owned a piece of land. Other-

Moulds for making tools and ornaments. Smith, son of Alfi and Amma in *The Song of Rig*, would have used moulds like these. They were discovered in Sweden. *(Statens Historiska Museet, Stockholm; Werner Forman Archive)*

wise he was obliged to hire his services or become a tenant-farmer. Karls were farmers, craftsmen, pedlars, and soldiers. They were the backbone of Scandinavia. They might be impoverished, barely richer than the thralls, or they might be very well-to-do. They had protection under the law and could vote on matters of public moment at an assembly, or *thing*. A thing was a meeting of free men to discuss law, religion, politics, or policy. Matters as important as the election or approval of a king came within its

scope. Originally these gatherings were the calling together of the karls in a given locality, probably as a marshalling for war. In time, however, they assumed the role of a forum for general debate.

Above the karls was the ruling caste, the jarls, who were essentially warriors. Their younger members would have raised bands of karls for trading and raiding expeditions. The greater karls gathered more permanent forces and exercised authority over a defined territory. Prior to 1000 it started to be customary for jarls to hold land from a king. This semi-feudal move was connected with the growing power of the monarchy, a symptom of increasing centralization within Scandinavian society. The process was abetted by the Christian Church, which preferred an alliance with a strong central authority, and the merchant guilds, which sought to restrict the enterprise of the free-booter. Yet in the Viking age there were few overall monarchs. Kings had to gain popular acclaim at all the things within their dominions. Local sentiment and aristocratic rivalries gave plenty of room for disruption, intrigue and reversals. A Swedish law states that the ruler 'shall not break the true laws of the land'. Approval was obviously a matter of importance to jarls, whatever their aspirations.

A king was, in pagan times, regarded as god-descended. His prestige would have been measured in terms of the number and effectiveness of his long-ships. He employed his navy to exact tribute, engage in profitable trade, and to undertake raids. Control of the sea-lanes permitted the king to enjoy his own estates in peace, for inevitably he would have been the greatest landowner. Without a capital he would have travelled from estate to estate in the company of his personal body-guard, men who swore loyalty unto death. These followers were similar to the warriors of the greater jarls.

Bone combs of the Viking period. Modir, in *The Song of Rig*, would have combed her tresses with such a comb. *(Museum of National Antiquities, Stockholm; Photoresources)*

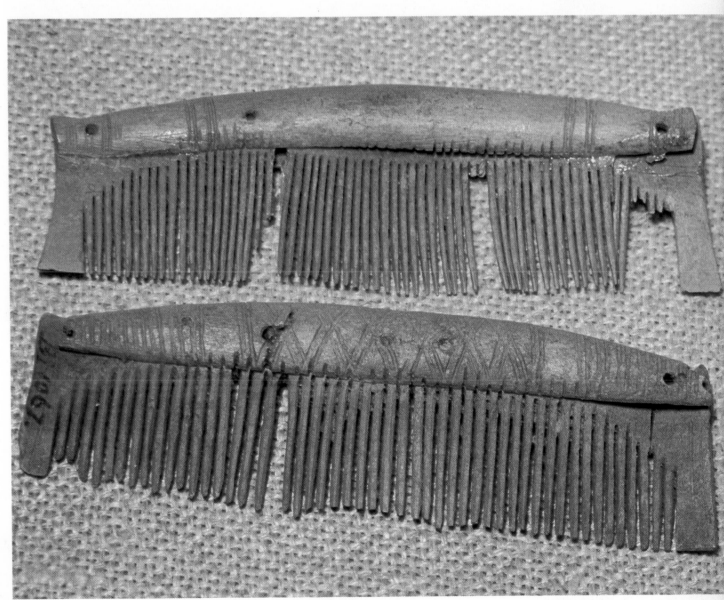

A Danish forge stone, part of the equipment belonging to a Viking smith. *(Artius Museum, Denmark; Werner Forman Archive)*

They were equipped, supported, and rewarded for their devotion and service. The royal revenues derived from a number of sources: the royal estates, forfeited property, tribute, booty, and trade. But the bulk of a ruler's wealth continued to be bound up with his own farms and woodland long after the Viking raids ceased.

Farming was in fact becoming more sophisticated. In Norway, cattle were transferred to high pasture-lands during summer months, and generally better breeding helped livestock to resist the harsh winters. Sheep proved the hardiest animals, especially in newly colonized Iceland. It was normal practice to keep animals in barns till spring. Settlement in Scandinavia changed only slowly from the pre-Viking norm of farmsteads. Villages and towns, where they did grow up, usually had a trading function in response to the expansion of the economy. Diet consisted of milk, meat, fish, bread, porridge, vegetables, fruit, and beer. Edible seaweed was also eaten in Iceland. At Lindholm Høje an inundation of sand has preserved a ploughed field, but the settlement there, comprising a large village, housed both farmers and metalworkers. Dwellings were small huts with sunken floors, bigger buildings of rectangular and rounded shape, and a courtyard house. In Iceland archaeologists have traced several farmsteads where, because of the inclement weather, outbuildings were linked to the main structure. They were constructed in wood, then covered in a thick layer of earth and finished with turf. One found at Gjaskogar had four sections; a hall 20 feet (six metres) long, with a hearth in the middle of the floor and beds along the walls; a living-room with a hearth and benches; a dairy with a sunken vat; and a toilet.

In contrast with the scattered farms of the period stand the four Danish military camps at Trelleborg, Aggersborg, Fyrkat, and Nonnebakken. They were all erected within the period 970–1020, and these strongholds conform to a pattern of barracks sited within a rampart. Trelleborg, in western Zealand, was planted on a defensive position between two navigable streams. Its most imposing feature

Detail of a Scandinavian ship, from a Gotland picture stone. The big rectangular sail, the chief means of propulsion, would have been made of heavy woollen cloth strengthened by rope. *(Statens Historiska Museum, Stockholm; Werner Forman Archive)*

25

An old turf-covered farmhouse in Iceland. Excavation at Gjaskogar reveals that the Vikings introduced this method of insulation against the cold. *(C. M. Dixon)*

is a circular bank, over 500 feet (152 metres) in diameter and 16 feet (5 metres) high. The bank is pierced by four entrances pointing in the direction of the points of the compass. Beyond it is a ditch on what used to be the landward side, and an outer bailey. Excavation has shown that enormous timber palisades and gateways completed the encampment's defences. Inside the circular rampart are the remains of sixteen longhouses with bowed sides, while the outer bailey contains fifteen more as well as a small cemetery. It has been estimated that

8000 big trees were needed for Trelleborg's construction. Altogether the camps could accommodate 4000 troops. They are testimony to the level of organization and discipline in the forces that devastated England at the time of Ethelred the Unready.

Throughout the Viking period trade prospered. Towns began to develop as places of exchange. These marketplaces, however, were invariably sited away from the coast and the attention of pirates. With good reason the Scandinavian farmer was advised, in the literature of wisdom, not to work far from his weapons. Marauders were commonplace, especially when the local jarls struggled with each other for supremacy. Swedish trading towns of Helgö and Birka stood on inland lakes, the Danish Lindolm Høje and Hedeby on narrow inlets. Helgö, an island in Lake Mäler not far from modern Stockholm, is the first settlement that can be identified as having primarily a commercial function. Founded in the fifth century, Helgö was a source of wealth and power to the Uppland royal house for nearly four hundred years. It was eclipsed towards the end of the eighth century by the neighbouring town of Birka. During its heyday Helgö was a centre of international trade and a centre of industry, producing rope and bronze jewellery. On the site a sixth-century bronze figure of the Buddha has been found. How this masterpiece found its way from distant India or Afghanistan we can only speculate.

In the ninth century Birka was one of the chief marts of Scandinavia. It traded with northern Scandinavia, Russia, southern Scandinavia, Germany, Frisia and England. The 32 acre (13 hectare) site at first appears to have been undefended, but some time in the ninth and tenth centuries the landward approach was safeguarded by a bank and ditch. There were probably timber barriers along the top of the bank and timber towers at the gateways. Dominating the entire settlement was a fortress built on a low hill outside the line of the enclosure. A beacon site hints at the careful scrutiny kept over merchant ships sailing up the 30 miles (48 kilometres) of twisting waterways from the open sea. Virtually all of the space within the defences was occupied. The garrison itself seems to have lived in barracks between the fortress and the town wall.

A model of the great Danish fortress at Trelleborg constructed 970–1020. From here the troops of Svein Forkbeard sailed to invade England. (*Photoresources*)

Over two thousand graves are reported in the vicinity and archaeologists have unearthed grave goods unparalleled in any other Viking settlement. Wealth derived almost exclusively from trade, in particular with the regions of the Volga. Muslim coins are seven times more numerous than Christian equivalents. Surrounded by the estates of the Uppland kings, Birka was obviously under royal patronage and protection. Its laws were framed in such a way as to guarantee the life and property of anyone who chose to take up residence. The town declined around 1000 as a result of the disruption of Russian commerce. Thereafter Gotland assumed prominence in northern Scandinavia.

Even bigger than Birka was Hedeby, a trading station of the Danes on the edge of northern Germany. The town existed from the eighth till the eleventh centuries. Hedeby failed to recover from the attack of Harald Hardradi the Ruthless, King of Norway, who sacked it in 1050 during one of his campaigns against the Danes. A raid by the Slavs in 1066 delivered the *coup de grâce*.

The Danes may have called the town Hedeby, 'the town of the hearths', because of its craftsmen's quarter. Unlike Birka, Hedeby was an important manufacturing centre. Its craftsmen were potters, weavers, jewellers, carvers in bone and horn, and workers in bronze and iron. There was also a mint. The area enclosed by the rampart was 60 acres (24 hectares); three gateways or tunnels interrupted the 1200 yards (1100 metres) sweep of the 30 feet (9 metres) high earthen embankment. A strongly built wooden mole, nearly 500 feet (152 metres) long, provided shelter for vessels and prevented flooding of the foreshore. Apart from the streets leading to the gateways, which were comparatively straight, labyrinthine alleyways separated the thatched-roof buildings. Some were built simply with wattle and daub, others were stave-built with vertical planking.

Al-Tartushi, an Arab from Cordoba, visited Hedeby about 950 and thought that the town was rather mean. It could hardly be compared with the elegance and splendour of the Moorish cities of Spain. Al-Tartushi was appalled by the barbarity of worship, since it was the custom to hang sacrificial animals on stakes outside dwellings. He noted the staple diet was fish. He also observed that the inhabitants took advantage of the sea to drown unwanted children. What really aggravated him, however, was the singing he heard. It sounded like the barking of dogs, only much more beastly. An interesting observation he makes concerns the use of cosmetics. According to Al-Tartushi, the independently minded womenfolk put make-up around their eyes, as did their menfolk. The use of make-up to render themselves attractive would seem to contradict the ferocity of the Vikings, yet an echo of concern for good looks can be found in the writings of John of Wallingford. In Wessex, John tells us, the Danes were hated for their habit of combing their hair every day, taking a bath every Saturday, and changing their woollens at regular intervals. 'By many such frivolous devices, they set off their persons, and in this wise laid siege to the virtue of the women.' Evidently English ladies were susceptible to these unheard-of blandishments.

From Al-Tartushi's account of Hedeby it can be surmised that the Christian faith introduced by the Frankish missionary Anksar about 830 was hard put to it to supplant the native traditions of belief. Anksar had travelled to Hedeby in the company of merchants, being robbed of forty books by pirates as his companions were of most of their possessions. Given permission to preach by the local king, Anksar converted the leader of Hedeby's assembly, or thing. This wealthy citizen raised a church on his own property. A change of king led to the closure of the church, but

further visits by the missionary in 850 and 854 ensured the reopening. The addition of a bell points to its public acceptance. Yet the old ways of Hedeby were not so easily changed and we find Anksar's successor, Rimbert, busily ransoming Christian slaves in the market there.

The thing was the repository of accepted custom. The free men who gathered at its meetings determined the laws. At Hedeby they obviously disregarded religion when arriving at a man's status for a Christian could be a slave. The democratic tenor of Viking life can be discerned in an incident in Normandy. During a Danish raid the defenders asked to know the name of the chief attacker. 'We are all equal', came the reply. Jarls were jarls and karls were karls. This raiding party probably comprised the latter only; they were all free men. The laws governing everyday life in Scandinavia covered property, personal injury, public morality, public order, and holy places. For offences against the person there existed a scale of injury and penalties varied from the chopping off of fingers to the chopping off of heads. Heavy fines could also be imposed and charges for trespass or injury were calculated to ensure the security of free men.

We are best informed about the laws of Iceland. The setting up in 930 of the Althing, the national assembly, meant that 'thereafter men had but one law in the land'. The Icelandic Republic lasted till 1262–4. The lawspeaker of the Althing was the embodiment of the constitution and the legal code. Influence in public affairs depended on grounding in law as much as accomplishment with arms. Aristocratic Icelanders did, of course, rule through the Althing – this was the age of intense loyalty to chieftains – yet their rule depended on the goodwill and support of the free men to make it operate.

Although we shall investigate cosmology and mythology at length when discussing the Viking mind, this

A model of houses at Hedeby, the Danish trading station in northern Germany. The site was not abandoned until 1066.
(Photoresources)

29

survey of the Viking homeland would be incomplete without some treatment of indigenous religion, which served as a strong bond between the Scandinavian peoples. Until the conversion of the Danes, the Swedes and the Norwegians to Christianity, they worshipped a pantheon of gods who had their origins in the common Indo-European tradition. Hot-tempered, red-headed Thor was a version of the sky god, the thunderer: his peers were Jupiter, Zeus, Indra, and the Hittite weather god.

Though acknowledged as the arch-enemy of the frost giants, the destructive elements of the cold northern lands, Thor was in many respects – his strength, his size, his energy, his huge appetite – more like one of the giants than one of the gods. Two goats drew his chariot across the sky: their names were Toothgrinder and Toothgnasher. His three magic weapons were the hammer, really a thunderbolt; iron gauntlets with which he handled the hammer-shaft; and a belt enabling him to increase his strength and his size by half. Adam of Bremen wrote in 1200 that three deities were reverenced in the great temple at Uppsala. 'Thor, the mightiest of the three,' he records, 'stands in the centre of the building, with Wodan and Fricco on his right and left. Thor, they say, holds the dominion of the air. He rules over thunder and lighting, winds and rain, clear weather and fertility . . . When plague or famine threatens, sacrifice is offered to Thor.'

Wodan is another name for Odin and probably meant wild or furious. One-eyed Odin inspired the frightful *berserkers*, the shield-biting warriors who rushed unheeding and naked into the midst of the fray. As Valfadir, 'father of the slain', he adopted as sons all the casualties of battle: Valhalla, the hall of the slain, was filled with the souls of champions gathered there by the Valkyries, female attendants who choose those fated to die. One of the soldiers in the army of the Norwegian king Harald the Ruthless dreamed of a Valkyrie shortly before his side was heavily defeated by King Harold at Stamford Bridge in 1066. He thought he was on the king's longship, and saw a great witch-wife standing on an island, with a fork in one hand to rake up the dead and a trough in the other to catch the blood. Fricco, also mentioned by Adam of Bremen, may have been Frey, the god of procreation.

The Vikings loved the heroic deeds of Thor, Odin, and the brother-sister deities, Frey and Freya. The emphasis on violence and valiant death chimed perfectly with the turbulent times. Yet the Viking outlook was permeated with an overwhelming sense of gloom. Evil was at work in the universe and the destruction of the world at hand. The fatalistic warriors of the longships were fascinated by the idea of *ragnarok*, the destruction of the gods, whom they believed would be consumed by fire and water in the middle of a battle between the two factions of the gods, supported by the slain, and the forces of evil, and led by the trickster-god Loki.

Scandinavian religion never approximated to an organized church. There were holy places – sacred rocks, altars, temples – and there were men who undertook the duties of priests, but no uniform theology emerged, nor any set procedures for worship. Religious belief was an individual affair. This diversity is reflected in the variety of funeral rites. Bodies might be cremated or buried in the earth; graves might be stone or wooden chambers, earth mounds or level places; and grave goods might include real ships and lavish provision for the after-life, or nothing at all. The coming of Christianity simplified burial. The Church forbade the bestowal of offerings since it did not insist that a person's status would remain the same for all eternity. The karl required neither his weapons nor his implements after death. The doctrine proved helpful in spreading the Christian faith among the Northmen.

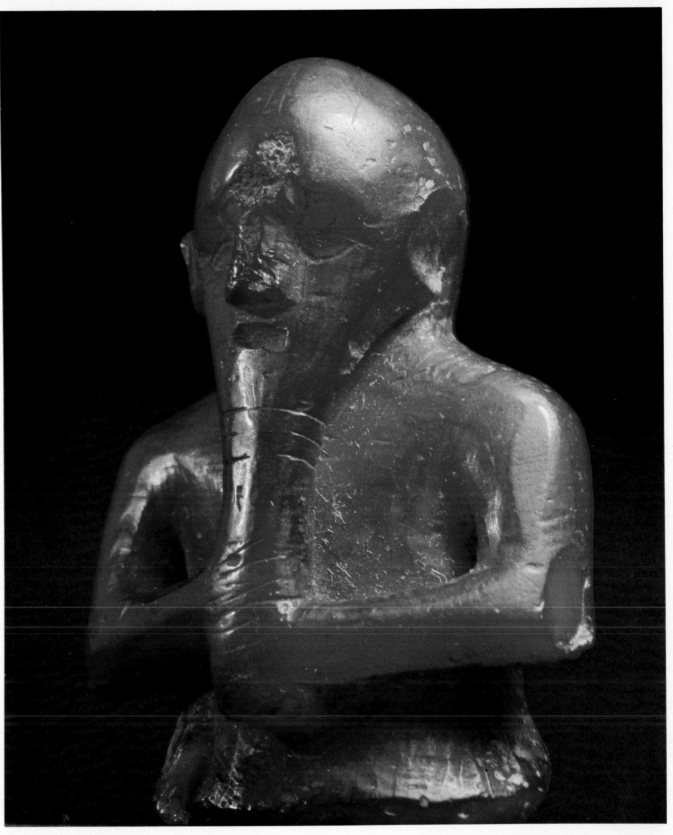

An amber carving of Thor, the Norse god of thunder. In his gauntletted hands he holds his thunder hammer, the scourge of the frost giants. *(National Museum Copenhagen; Werner Forman Archive)*

The Viking Onslaught

The Vikings impressed themselves on the minds of their contemporaries and later generations as implacable warriors. 'A hundred hard-steeled iron heads on one neck, and a hundred sharp, ready, cool, never-rusting, brazen tongues in each head, and a hundred talkative, loud, unceasing voices from each tongue,' an Irish chronicler protests, 'could not recount or narrate, number or tell, what all the Irish suffered.' The Viking onslaught was of spectacular impact because it occurred after two hundred hundred years of comparative calm, the seventh and eighth centuries. The dust had settled after the collapse of the western provinces of the Roman Empire and a new order had emerged. Under Charlemagne the Franks reconquered much of the old Roman dominion and annexed the majority of lands inhabited by the Germans. Charlemagne's authority ran from the Pyrenees in the west to the Elbe in the east, from the Frisian coast in the north to Monte Cassino in the south. The coronation of Charlemagne by the Pope in Rome on Christmas Day 800 appeared to signalize a return to unity and peace.

It was during this apparently peaceful period that the Viking raids started, heralded by the sacking of the monastery of St Cuthbert at Lindisfarne in 793. Situated on an exposed island off the coast of Northumberland, the famous foundation was a sitting target for a lightning attack. France, Ireland and Wales also experienced the fury of the sea-raiders. Soon nowhere seemed out of their bloody reach. How was it that the Vikings became so threatening? The straightforward answer is nautics. The Scandinavian shipwrights had brought to perfection the longship. Easy to manoeuvre, the average vessel measured about 75 feet (23 metres) from stem to stern, 18 feet (5.5 metres) in beam, and 6 feet (2 metres) from keel to gunwale. Above all the very shallow draught, hardly ever more than 4 feet (120 centimetres), allowed its steersman to follow the course of even shallow rivers. Equipped with oars and a sail, the longship could dash from one unexpected spot to another with great speed. Larger craft may have been in commission too. There is mention of one vessel with a complement of two hundred men. But it was the long ship that the tough farmer-fishermen of Scandinavia sailed in search of land and plunder. Their nautical skills – accumulated over centuries of coastal sailing – gave these rovers the command of the seas and the capacity to mount sea-borne expeditions. Experience of ocean navigation led to an understanding of latitude, making possible the voyages to distant Iceland, Greenland, and America. The average longship had a crew of about thirty-two men.

The raids in the final decade of the eighth century were a prelude to the more widespread and coordinated onslaught in the ninth. From opportunist attack the Vikings progressed to large-scale invasion, conquest, colonization, and trade. What were the reasons for this course of events?

OPPOSITE: the restored Gokstad ship indicates the skill with which Viking craftsmen built their longships. Combining speed and stability at sea with the ability to sail in shallow waters, they proved most effective raiding vessels. *(University Museum of National Antiquities, Oslo, Norway)*

First, there was the diminution of conflict in Scandinavia. As we saw in the last chapter, the modern states of Norway, Denmark, and Sweden were there in embryo. The rise of kings, acknowledged by jarls and karls, helped remove internal quarrels, so encouraging the more spirited warriors to look beyond the seas for adventure and gain. Overpopulation and land-shortage were certainly sharp spurs. The prizes of wealth, slaves, and fame would have appealed strongly to impoverished aristocrats and free men. In addition, the success of the early raids themselves must have been a powerful stimulus. Longships returned home laden with gold, silver, and precious stones, stripped from scarcely defended churches, monasteries, and nunneries. The temptation to grasp more was always present. Impetus to Danish military adventure may have also come from Charlemagne's conquest of Saxony. The Danish reaction to the increasing pressure from the south was a blow at Frisia, a first step towards the rich southern lands of El Dorado.

The victims of the Vikings, and especially the clerics in isolated foundations, saw their aggressors as inhuman creatures. They were heathen. They had neither regard for human life nor feeling for human suffering. They took pleasure in inflicting death and destruction. They raped, captured, slew, burned and pillaged indiscriminately. No one could guess what their next atrocity might be. Their number and their swiftness defied understanding and their successes were legion. So the chroniclers and annalists, contemporary with the Viking period and after the raiding ceased, expressed the reaction of Christian Europe. These accounts of the Vikings have led historians to suppose huge fleets to have sailed in the attacks. Chroniclers

Sogne Fjord, Norway. The shortage of agricultural land in mountainous Scandinavia was a factor behind the Viking onslaught. *(Werner Forman Archive)*

35

Silver pendants depicting the hardbitten heroes of the Viking raids. They were discovered in Sweden. *(Statens Historiska Museet, Stockholm; Michael Holford Library)*

talked of hundreds of ships and thousands of men.

Today, it is appreciated that these figures are over-inflated – a consequence of shock and bewilderment perhaps. To keep an army together for a campaign, not to say a series of campaigns, would have demanded a feat of supply beyond Scandinavian means. Even the Franks were obliged to curtail the length of the fighting season because of the difficulties of feeding a large host and foraging for its mounts. The Danish fortresses of Trelleborg, Aggersborg, Fyrkat, and Nonnebakken indicate a measure of organization in the late tenth century that implies the raising of royal armies, yet the total number of troops could not have exceeded eight thousand. The four camps were designed for only half that number. And by this time the Viking period was drawing to a close. It would appear that few Vikings engaged in the early raids and that the number of participants only increased as colonization occurred. The late tenth-century Danish armies and the Norwegian armies of the early eleventh century

were exceptionally big and connected with the political ambitions of powerful kings. Indeed, the tactics of the Viking raids make sense only if the numbers taking part were comparatively small.

The Vikings themselves, of course, were hardbitten and they inhabited a world suited to fierce action. At its most extreme, the ruthlessness, fearlessness and violence of the Vikings were epitomised by the berserkers. These naked warriors foamed at the mouth, bit the edges of their shields, and fought as men possessed. Yet a longship of fierce, brave, hardy, greedy and unscrupulous warriors – a typical Viking crew – would have been a keen instrument of war in the hands of an able, cunning and daring leader. It could strike swiftly and mercilessly where least anticipated; it could join other craft in a sudden assault on a well-defended centre; and, when pressed by a local levy, it could escape by water or retreat behind the palisade of a raiding base. The tactics used on the southerners were those of the *strandhogg*, the quick-in, quick-out shore-raid perfected in the internecine conflicts of Scandinavia. A strandhogg was the traditional means of filling an empty larder. The gradual decline of this activity in northern waters under the influence of stronger rulers facilitated its transfer south.

The effectiveness of small bands of freebooters should not surprise us. Only the Frankish Empire possessed any unity, and by 843 its fragility was transparent. The territories which eventually formed the modern states of France and Germany were already drifting apart. In the tenth century the King of Germany and the duke of the Franks needed to speak through an interpreter. Scotland, Ireland, England, Wales, and Russia lacked even a semblance of unity. They comprised a patchwork of small kingdoms, usually engaged in border wars. In England the kingdom of Mercia gained a brief ascendancy under Offa (757–96), who built a dyke along the

A looted Irish
bishop's crozier,
unearthed at the
trading port of
Helgö in Sweden.
The easy success of
early Viking raids
helped stimulate
further attacks.
*(Statens Historiska
Museet, Stockholm;
Werner Forman
Archive)*

37

boundary of Wales to safeguard his western flank. He claimed to be *rex Anglorum*, King of the English, but within thirty years of his death the kingdom had disintegrated. Resistance to the Vikings was piecemeal till Alfred the Great, king of Wessex, introduced his military and naval reforms in the 890s. In particular, the establishment of a network of defences, small fortified settlements approximately 20 miles (32 kilometres) apart, served to protect a locality and hold up an attacker's advance.

In the 820s Viking raids intensified. 'The sea spewed forth floods of foreigners over Ireland,' says the *Annals of Ulster*, 'so that no harbour, no beach, no stronghold, no fort, no castle, might be found, but it was sunk beneath waves of northmen and pirates.' In 836 the Vikings set up a permanent raiding base on the site of modern Dublin, where a monastery already

stood. Then shortly before 840 the Norwegian war-leader Turgeis arrived with a fleet. Taking advantage of tribal rivalries, Turgeis managed to seize the Armagh, the ecclesiastical centre of Ireland. His forays soon extended southwards and westwards, bringing into his coffers untold riches. Turgeis determined to strengthen his position and become a king in his own right. Strongholds were built at Wexford, Waterford, Cork and Limerick, while the defences of Dublin were improved. Again with the help of tribal differences and possibly Irish apostates, Turgeis extended his domain across the island, desecrating Christian shrines as he went. His headlong career came to a watery close in 845: captured by an Irish monarch, he was drowned in a lough.

The loss of Turgeis put the Norwegian Vikings on the defensive and for five years the Irish pinned them down

ABOVE: One of two Irish defence towers at the monastic settlement of Clonmacnois. It was constructed in the tenth century to resist the Viking attack on Ireland. *(C. M. Dixon)*

OPPOSITE: The terrible Vikings. These robust chessmen come from a Viking hoard discovered on the Isle of Lewis in the Hebrides, and date from the eleventh or twelfth centuries. *(British Museum; Photoresources)*

39

A mounting from a Frankish sword belt. This piece of looted gold was found in a grave near modern Oslo, Norway. (*Universitetets Oldsaksamling, Oslo; Werner Forman Archive*)

in their base areas. The arrival of a fleet of Danes in 849 added to the confused struggle as these Vikings set upon the weakened Norwegians. They overran Dublin in 851, sank a Norwegian fleet off Carlingford in 852, and harried the surviving garrisons. The Irish were relieved to see the Northmen tearing each other to pieces, but their joy was shortlived. In 853 a new fleet commanded by a certain Olaf, a relation of Turgeis, restored Norwegian supremacy and those Danes who could not stomach his leadership quit Ireland for England. Olaf ruled till 871, when he returned to Norway and died in battle there. Ivar succeeded his brother Olaf and held on to the kingdom, though an Irish counter-attack captured Dublin in 902. Iceland, not Ireland was attracting Viking reinforcements just then.

During this period the English felt the wrath of the Danes. In 835, the *Anglo-Saxon Chronicle* reports, 'the heathen desecrated Sheppey'. On the continent too, Viking attacks were more frequent and more injurious. Frisia was ravaged and in 834 the town of Dorestad sacked. This premier trading-port on the Rhine had strong

defences and a Frankish fortress nearby. Next Noirmoutier in Aquitaine was fired. The range of strikes was widening: Rouen, Paris, London, Cornwall, Normandy, Kent, Hamburg and Nantes. The slaughter on 24 June 842 in Nantes surpassed belief. It was the feast of St John and the streets were crowded with pilgrims. Thousands died that day, the bishop of the city included. The Norwegian ships sailed back down the Loire brimming with booty. More threatening still the Vikings began to winter in raiding bases, like the one they established on the island of Noirmoutier. In England, the *Anglo-Saxon Chronicle* notes, on Thanet in 850 'the heathen for the first time remained over the winter'. So humiliated were the Franks after their poor efforts to defend Paris that they actually offered the raiders 7000 pounds of silver to depart. The bribe was a portent. Later Vikings would look for the same again.

So adventurous did the Viking raiders become in these years that a fleet dared to enter the Guadalquivir river and assault the Moorish city of Seville. Except for its citadel, the Vikings were in control for a week. Their impudence, however, did not go unpunished. The Moors retaliated swiftly, cutting off raiding parties, capturing raiders, and firing boats. Viking prisoners were soon hanging from the palm trees of Seville, the city's gallows being overloaded. At last the exhausted Danes ransomed their prisoners for food and clothes, then set sail for home. The year was 844.

A decade later another fleet raided south, attacking the North African and Spanish coastlines before striking at southern France. The towns of Arles, Nîmes, and Valence were all pillaged. A Frankish rally drove the Vikings off, and Hastein, their leader, led them on to Pisa and Rome. Pisa presented few problems but Hastein judged the seat of St Peter to be too strongly defended for direct assault. His cunning brain devised a trick.

Pretending to be dead, his men asked that the chieftain be allowed a Christian burial within the walls. This was granted. At the graveside Hastein awoke, his men drew their swords, and the citizens were overcome. But Hastein's joy turned to anger on learning that he was mistaken and that the city was not Rome at all. He ordered its annihilation. We hear of further activities in the Western Mediterranean such as an attack on Navarre and a defeat near Gibralter. Hastein was the archetypal early Viking, a foolhardy opportunist.

In the 860s the character of raiding changed. Attacks became more sustained and the raiders lived off the invaded land for a longer time. A Viking army overcame the Northumbrians at York in 867 and permanently occupied the city. Two years later a contingent marched down through Mercia to East Anglia. King Edmund was killed, his forces routed, and the people enslaved. In 870 the Danes moved unsuccessfully against Wessex, the Saxons winning a victory at Ashdown in Berkshire. The new king of Wessex, Alfred, was instrumental in this reverse. He could do nothing, however, for the Mercians, who collapsed in 874. The Danish occupation was strengthened by large numbers of settlers in the so-called Five Boroughs – Lincoln, Derby, Nottingham, Leicester and Stamford. The Five Boroughs became Danish and there is evidence of Danes settling in the countryside, often on previously untilled land. The boundary between the Danes and the English was thus the Roman road to Watling Street.

By 878 the Danish leaders were ready to try out the English again, Gloucester and Chippenham falling. Alfred rallied the Saxons, yet the treaty of 886 confirmed the Danelaw, the Viking-held area of eastern and northern England. The Saxon King was obliged to acknowledge the presence of a powerful and hostile neighbour. Its sole advantage was a respite, for the Danish colonization of half of England turned the attention of the more belligerent Vikings to the continent, where the dismemberment of the Frankish Empire offered rich pickings. The Frankish kings were reluctant to contest the passage of the raiders – dynastic squabbles inclined them to favour the inducement of silver, much prized in Scandinavia. Thousands of pounds of silver were paid over to the Vikings.

Alfred used the interregnum to good purpose. When the fighting was renewed, the English were ready to meet the Danes on land and sea. Alfred reorganized his forces to gain

Viking weapons from Yorkshire. The settlement of East Anglia, Mercia and Northumberland was accomplished by well-armed Vikings. *(Yorkshire Museum; photo: Clive Friend, FIIP, Woodmansterne Ltd.)*

An amulet of Thor's hammer, from Denmark. Lucky charms would have been worn by soldiers in Svein Forkbeard's invasion force. At the battle of Hastings even the Christian duke William wore relics sent to him by the Pope. *(National Museum, Copenhagen; Photoresources)*

mobility, the asset exploited by the Vikings. The *Anglo-Saxon Chronicle* informs us that he 'divided his levies into two sections, so that there was always half at home and half on active service, with the exception of those whose duty it was to man the fortresses.' These *burghs*, fortified settlements, formed a network of sanctuaries for village folk during an invasion. They were maintained at local expense for the sake of the locality. They also acted as a break on an invader's movements. Alfred's last innovation was the building of a navy.

The campaign of 892–6 was decisive. It established that the whole of England would not fall at once into Viking hands. The Saxons matched the Danish armies and, in the English Channel, Alfred's sailors even dispersed a flotilla of six longships. The wretched Viking prisoners were strung up at Winchester like common thieves. Alfred's successor, Edward the Elder (899–924), was able to bring the whole of the Danelaw south of the river Humber under English rule. Yet the attitude of the Vikings themselves was changing, as a desire to settle overtook the desire to raid. Only in the eleventh century would Danish armies return in strength to England. This conquest would be of a different type, an annexation for political and

economic reasons.

Across the Channel other Vikings, whether of Danish or Norwegian descent we do not know, had gained possession of Normandy. The Franks had ceded this province in 911, possibly with the hope that its Northmen settlers would assist in the guarding of the coastline. Their chieftain was named Rollo. He did homage to the Frankish ruler and was baptised. In his arrangement of the principality he disclosed an un-Scandinavian tendency towards feudalism. He forbade 'things' and land was parcelled out to his principal followers. Within three generations the Viking element had been submerged by Frankish customs and language. Norman-French was the tongue of William the Conqueror in 1066.

The confidence of the English Kings is attested by Edgar's decree of 962. It recognised the right of Danish subjects to their own legal and social customs. It institutionalized the Danelaw. King Edgar appreciated the general wish for peace and the improved relations between the English and the Danes. At his court were lords of both peoples. The peace ended in 980 during the reign of Ethelred the Unready. The first Viking raids were a repetition of the sudden descents on the coast of Wessex by the early seekers of plunder. But after the accession of Svein Forkbeard Haraldsson to the Danish throne in 985 the situation altered dramatically. Svein Forkbeard made up his mind to subdue England. Between 1003 and 1005 his army sacked Exeter, Wilton, Salisbury, Norwich and Thetford. In 1006 it campaigned from its bases on the Isle of Wight and at Reading. Bribes bought off the Danes till 1009, when Svein Forkbeard's fleet anchored off Sandwich. The Danish army was by now a standing one, as we have seen from the military fortresses like Trelleborg. To maintain it the Danish king needed regular English bribes or regular English revenues and it could be argued that King Ethelred's gifts of silver paid the troops who eventu-

ally defeated him. Enormous hoards of Anglo-Saxon coins in Scandinavia underline this ironic transaction. By 1014 the pretence was no longer necessary: Ethelred had fled to the continent and the people accepted Svein Forkbeard as king. His son Knut secured the realm following his death that year. He was proclaimed ruler immediately after gaining a crushing victory in 1016 at Ashingdon in Essex. In 1018–19 he succeeded to the Danish throne on the death of his brother. By 1028 Knut's enterprise in Scandinavia had made him *rex totius Angliae et Denmarchiae et Norregiae et partis Slavorum*. He ruled the peoples of England, Denmark, Norway and Skane. It was a great Danish Empire.

In England the reign of Knut, or Canute the Great as he is sometimes termed, was not unwelcome. The years of battle ceased and law and order returned. Like the Saxon Edgar, Knut treated as far as practical Danes and English alike. His own enactments were based on Edgar's code and his patronage of the Church allayed the fears of the faithful. When he died in 1035 at the age of forty, he was solemnly interred in the Saxon royal church at Winchester and not

The martyrdom of King Edmund in 870. A fifteenth century wall-painting in the church of St Peter and St Paul at Pickering, North Yorkshire. *(Photoresources)*

taken back to his native Denmark. The lack of distinguished heirs afflicted England as much as Denmark. While the Viking Normandy cast covetous eyes on English shores, the Norwegians under Harald the Ruthless ravaged the Danish homeland. In the last chapter we encountered this blood-thirsty Norwegian king, burning the commercial centre of Hedeby in 1050. It was entirely in character. In many ways he was the last truly Viking leader, almost a throw-back to the earlier days of plunder and terror. The ruthless raider was an anachronism at home and abroad, for Scandinavia and its overseas colonies were now predominantly settled with farmers and traders.

In 1066 Harald the Ruthless contested the English throne. He knew William, Duke of Normandy, intended to depose Harold Godwinson the Englishman and therefore he acted with haste. Sailing up the Humber and the Ouse to York, he defeated the forces gathered there and was warmly received in the city. But at Stamford Bridge, the *Anglo-Saxon Chronicle* relates, 'a stubborn battle was fought . . . and there Harald king of Norway slain.' The English army, victorious but scathed, had to hasten south to face at Hastings the other Viking contender, William. There it met complete defeat. The mounted Normans overwhelmed the English foot soldiers. The Norman conquest, it might be said, was indirectly a final Viking triumph. Yet the old customs of the Northmen had already been superseded by those of the Normans. The notion of free men and the right of free speech had been submerged beneath a centralized military administration. Feudalism was come from France.

The Bayeux tapestry features Viking-style ships from Normandy, which was ceded to the Vikings in 911. Although the Viking lifestyle was gradually submerged by Frankish customs, traces of its influence still remained in 1066. *(Michael Holford Library)*

HIC EXEVNT: CABALL

Viking Colonization and Exploration

The *Anglo-Saxon Chronicle* draws a distinction about the Vikings in England. It refers to Danes and Danes 'with stock'. Those with cows and sheep were neither the marauders of the early raids nor the full-time soldiers of the late invading armies: they were colonists, farmers settled in the Danelaw. The colonization movement, which had commenced before the raids at the end of the eighth century, gained momentum once piracy became less easy and the new lands in the Atlantic were discovered. The Orkneys were first settled around 780 and longships reached the Faroes and Iceland by around 800. The explorers and migrants were principally Norwegians and Danes. As we shall see in the next chapter, the parallel movement of the Swedes took them eastwards to Russia.

The waters of the North Sea and the Atlantic Ocean invited the restless, impoverished and discontented. The advent of a stronger monarchy in Norway and Denmark did not suit everyone. The sturdy independence of the settlers in Iceland led them by 930 to found a republic. They would have no truck with kings. The land-hungry Vikings liked the new lands they reached. Reports carried back to Scandinavia encouraged further waves of migration. By the end of the tenth century seventy or eighty thousand people had arrived in Iceland.

The Lindisfarne raid of 793 may have been an opportunist move by Vikings involved in the settlement of the Scottish isles, the Orkneys, Shetlands and Hebrides. The earliest settlements on the isles, founded in the 780s, appear to have been peaceful and carried out by men concerned to find pastureland, but some of the crews in the longships might have had an interest in plunder too. Typical of the settlements there is the farmstead of

The 'canal' built by the Vikings near the promontory fort at Ruadha a' Dunain on the Isle of Skye, Scotland. The water-way allowed the Viking longships access to a small loch. (*C. M. Dixon*)

47

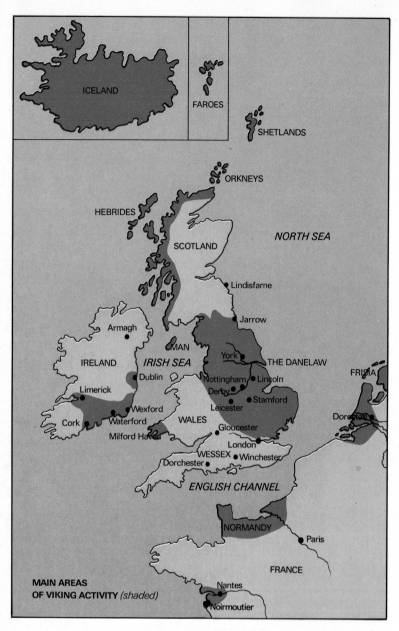

MAIN AREAS
OF VIKING ACTIVITY *(shaded)*

main areas of colonization, as opposed to conquest, were explored and occupied. Intense was the feeling of the Vikings for the land they settled on. They transferred from Scandinavia the forest-clearer's pride in his estate. The joy of the first migrants to Iceland knew no bounds. The bleak and almost treeless island was described as a veritable paradise – every blade of grass dripped with butter. The Faroes, or Sheep Islands, and Iceland were settled in the 860s and the 870s. Both had already been visited, and lived on, by Irish hermits, men who had 'turned their back on Ireland'. The founding-father of Iceland was Ingolf Arnarson. In 874 he built his farm amid the hot springs of Reykjavik, the modern capital. According to the *Landnáma-bók*, the Book of Settlements, Ingolf was the first Norwegian who 'took land into his possession'. Settlement on the empty island was purely a matter of personal initiative. Good planning, of course, was very necessary, otherwise an expedition could get into desperate straits. Ships had to be constructed and fitted out; provisions, tools and weapons gathered; livestock, seeds and slaves collected; and families as well as retainers organized. To prepare for such a venture a Viking household had to be fairly wealthy. It is likely that loot from pirate raids provided the financial backing required. The power-ful king of Norway, Harald Fairhair, tried to exercise some control over the settlement of Iceland, but at such a distance it is doubtful if his pro-nouncements held sway. The *Land-námabók* says that he made an attempt to limit family holdings. He decreed that 'no one should occupy more than he and his crew could carry fire round in one day.'

Ingolf Arnarson made a reconnais-sance to Iceland before returning to Norway to plan a permanent settle-ment. On the second voyage to the island he felt himself to be under the special protection of Thor, whom he vowed should lead him to whatever he

OPPOSITE:
Thingvellir, or Parliament Plains, where the national assembly of Iceland met from 930 to 1262–4. The Althing was the deliberative body of the Icelandic Republic. (*Werner Forman Archive*)

Jarlshof, Shetland. The ninth-century complex has a farmhouse, a bath-house, a smithy, a barn, a cattle-pen, and an outhouse possibly for slaves. The long, aisled farmhouse contains a living room with a hearth and sleeping berths, and a kitchen. Animals kept were sheep, cows, pigs, and chicken. But the inhabitants supplemented their home-grown plant and animal food with catches of fish and hunted meat. The bones of deer, seals, whales, and cod are in evidence.

From the Scottish isles the Nor-wegians sailed to Ireland, where in 836 a permanent base was established at Dublin. They also sailed westwards to the Faroes and beyond. By 860 the

was to settle. He cast overboard a piece of furniture and afterwards settled where it washed ashore. Yet the landing was not without incident. Ingolf had to put down an insurrection of his Irish slaves, who killed many of the Vikings. The Irish hermits and anchorites living on Iceland were less pugnacious – they quietly and quickly departed. Other expeditions of Viking settlers followed Ingolf and within a year or two local customs and laws came into being. The direction of affairs was in the hands of the chieftains of the scattered communities. In 930 these local leaders joined themselves together to form a national assembly, the Althing, held for two weeks every year. Though the chieftains ran the Althing, membership was granted to all free men who chose or were asked to join in its deliberations. The legal code established by the assembly was modelled on the laws of Norway. A certain Ulfljot was sent back to Scandinavia to devise a suitable adaptation. Unfortunately the code is now lost.

At a meeting of the Althing in 1000 two Christian missionaries spoke. The subsequent argument between their followers and the worshippers of Thor and Odin compelled the lawspeaker Thorgeir to intervene. He made the assembly promise to accept his ruling. 'If the laws are divided,' Thorgeir is reputed to have said, 'the peace will be divided and we cannot tolerate that.' In the event, a day's consideration persuaded him to side with the Christians. Although the pagans were upset by the judgement, the Christian faith became law. The authority of the remarkable national assembly – for such it really was – continued down the centuries to 1262–4, when the Norwegian king Hakon gained possession of the island.

The tenth and eleventh centuries in Iceland constituted the age of the sagas. These heroic poems, written down in the thirteenth century, recount the heady years of the Icelandic Republic. They tell of larger-than-life

men and women, grim battles and bitter feuds, trusted companions and treacherous relations, daring exploits and low cunning. A classic figure is the famous Njal. His only peculiarity was the inability to grow a beard. Rich, handsome, brave, Njal the warrior-chieftain was 'outstandingly skilful with arms'. Our presentday knowledge of Viking religion and mythology owes an immense debt to the work of the Icelandic scholar and statesman Snorri Sturluson (1179–1241), whose *Prose Edda* comprises a handbook for poets on the world of the heathen gods, providing explanations of metaphors based on the old myths.

The coast of Greenland is closer to Iceland than the Faroes. Not many years passed before accidental landfalls were made on Greenland, though not until 982 was a thorough exploration mounted. In that year Eirik the Red, outlawed from Iceland and Norway for murder, decided to use his three-year banishment exploring the Atlantic ocean westward. As a result, he reached the empty Greenland coast and staked his claim to the best land he found there. When he returned to Iceland after three years, he found that famine disposed many people to sail back with him. Twenty-five vessels set out in 986. Eirik's holdings were sited on the southern tip of Greenland, around Eiriksfjord. Later settlement also occurred farther north, and the total population exceeded three thousand. The Greenlanders traded furs, hides, ropes, oil, woollens and sea-ivory in exchange for corn, iron and timber. They remained independent till the Norwegian annexation of 1261.

The Greenlanders explored the seas around them, but the first voyage to America was unplanned. In 985–6 Bjarni Herjolfsson, sailing to join his father in the Greenland settlements,

Godafoss in Northern Iceland where Thorgeir, who was responsible for accepting Christianity into Iceland around 1000 AD, threw his pagan idols over the waterfall. (C. M. Dixon)

51

was blown off course and sighted North America. News of the unexpected discovery of wooded land with low hills excited Leif the Lucky, Eirik's son, who led a reconnaissance there about 990. Leif's ship reached present-day Canada and his crew put ashore in three places. Leif named them Helluland, Markland and Vinland. The first, Helluland or Flatstone Land, was the southern reach of Baffin Island, a desolate track. Markland or Wood Land, the second landing-place, was Labrador, its forested coastline furnished with sandy beaches. Lastly, Vinland or Wineland was probably the northern tip of Newfoundland. Leif and his companions were overjoyed with its wild grapes, grasses, trees and salmon. After wintering there, Leif returned to take up the leadership of the Greenland settlements, Eirik the Red having died, and the task of exploration fell to others. His own brother Thorvald was eager to go. The sagas recall that he was killed by an Indian arrow in a skirmish provoked by his men.

The saga version of Thorfinn Karlsefni's expedition shortly afterwards hints at permanent settlement. We learn that the Vikings took their women and cattle with them, and built timber houses close to a lake. The

Brattahild in Eiriksfjord, where the leaders of the Greenland community always lived. From here the voyages of discovery to Baffin Island and the eastern shores of Canada were made. *(Werner Forman Archive)*

situation was a southern one. 'No snow fell, and their entire stock found its food grazing in the open.' One spring morning an armada of skin-boats hove into view, carrying numerous Indian braves. Happily for the Vikings the visitors had come to trade furs. They wanted arms but were beguiled into drinking milk instead. However, the Vikings were soon under attack and after three winters they quit. Karlsefni recognised the manpower shortage that made the natives unbeatable. So far from Greenland and Iceland, not to say Scandinavia, the Vikings could not afford heavy casualties, especially as the weapons of both sides were quite evenly matched.

How historically accurate is such an account? The identity of Vinland has provoked much controversy. Questionable evidence has been produced this century to justify several theories. But a number of hard facts do exist. For instance, a reference to Vinland in the writings of Adam of Bremen is unimpeachable. He reports that he was told 'of yet another island, discovered by many in the ocean, which is called Wineland from the circumstance that vines grow there of their own accord, and produce fine wine. The abundance of unsown corn there we have learned, not from fabulous stories, but the testimony of worthy Danes.' A second piece of evidence comes from archaeological research. In the 1960s, excavations at L'Anse-aux-Meadows in the north of New-foundland revealed a site dated by the radio-carbon method to the Viking period. The complex of eight buildings is reminiscent of the farmsteads erected by the Vikings. A spindle-whorl recovered there confirms a Greenland influence.

The Greenland settlements themselves were not abandoned till the fifteenth century. Worsening climatic conditions from 1200 onwards made life harder. The medieval mini-ice age was in progress. Gradually the land turned into a habitat best suited to the

Eskimos who, around 1500, may have wiped out those descendants of the Viking settlers remaining. Presumably their inherited sense of attachment to the land proved stronger than a desire to escape. The end of the Greenland colonization must forever remain wreathed in cold uncertainty.

As mentioned above, Norwegian penetration from the Scottish isles reached down to Ireland, the Isle of Man and Wales. The Danes tended to approach British shores directly across the North Sea. The Isle of Man was a target for raids from the late eighth century onwards. When the tide of raiders turned into a tide of colonists in the early tenth century,

A bronze bird of Odin, possibly a raven. This ceremonial stick-top would have belonged to a prominent person, like the legendary Njal. It was found in Sweden. *(Statens Historiska Museet, Stockholm; Werner Forman Archive)*

the island was taken over by emigrants from Viking settlements in Scotland and Ireland. Not that this prevented Svein Forkbeard from pillaging the islanders in 994. The strategic situation of the island, midway between northern England and Ireland, ensured frequent attention. Had the Viking dominion lasted in both countries it might have been the link between two halves of a new Viking state. The recovery of the Irish after 900 put an end to this possibility, as did the revival of English fortunes during the reign of Alfred the Great.

The Irish overran the great Viking base of Dublin in 902, forcing many Norwegians to seek their fortune in Mercia and Northumbria. The Irish could not dislodge the invaders without a prolonged struggle: the Vikings were back in 914, recovered Dublin, and initiated another century of strife. The very factions in Irish politics, whereby some Irishmen would side with the Norwegians and others bitterly oppose them, meant that events went by twists and turns. At the battle of Clontarf, near Dublin, in 1014, the Viking host was put to

rout yet in both ranks were Norwegians and Irish. This mingling of peoples and interests explains why Viking settlers were not immediately expelled from Ireland. They stayed on in the towns as traders, to the benefit of the island's economy.

The story of the Vikings in Wales is quite distinct. There the activities of the invaders and settlers were essentially peripheral. The Welsh chroniclers, like the English, regarded them as one people – *y Normanyeit Duon*, the Black Norsemen. In the *Welsh Annals* are recorded an unsuccessful Viking attack on the Gower peninsular in 860, depredations in Dyfed in 877, and the assault across the river Severn in 893. Like their Celtic kinsmen of Cornwall and Strathclyde, the Welsh were ambivalent about the Vikings. Lurking beneath the surface of their complaints about intrusion was a profound anti-Saxon sentiment. If they were to let the Anglo-Saxons take the brunt of the Viking onslaught, there would be a possibility that, sufficiently weakened, they might be driven away with Celtic help. The

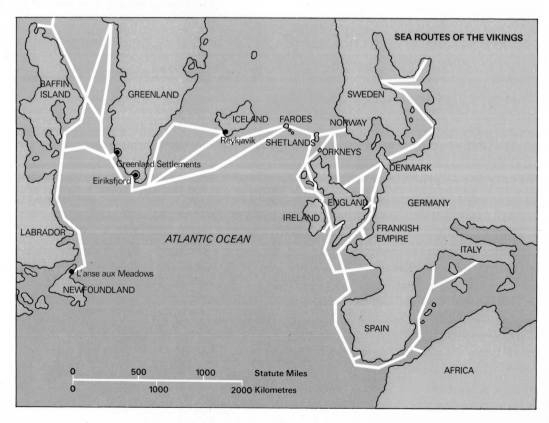

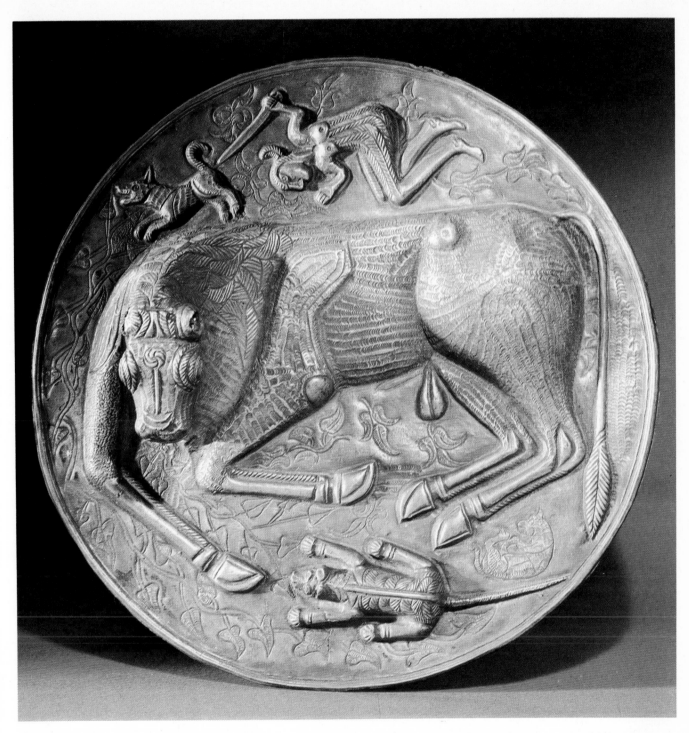

dreamed of Celtic-Viking alliance never materialized. Within both peoples there were too many divisions. We do find, though, around Milford Haven a number of Viking settlements, the inhabitants of which seem finally to have merged with the local population.

Intermarriage and social intercourse occurred also within the Danelaw. The English and the Danes were not so far removed in terms of language, the interchange of tongues being well advanced before the death of Knut in 1035. Common words adopted by the English language from the Vikings are law, husband, fellow, awkward, happy, ill, odd, loose, ugly, wrong, leg, calf, bull, egg, bank, skin, skull, knife and window. The occupation of East Anglia from 879 onwards reveals the conciliatory mood of the Danes. After defeat by Alfred at Eddington the previous year, the

The circular base of a Celtic cauldron, dating from 100 BC. Made of silver-gilt, this masterpiece was probably looted from Ireland during the Viking era. It was found in Denmark. *(National Museum, Copenhagen; Werner Forman Archive)*

Danish leader Guthram agreed by the treaty of Wedmore to withdraw his forces from Wessex and accept baptism himself. However nominal his conversion to Christianity, the acceptance of the Church by Guthram ensured religious toleration for English subjects inside the boundaries of the lands he held in East Anglia.

Under 'Guthram's Peace', as it was not ungratefully called, English and Danes were ranked alike. It would be cynical to suggest that the Vikings turned to farming only when the devastation of England was so extensive that the old-style raids were no longer profitable. As we have seen in Iceland, the Vikings settled down as farmers quickly if there was an absence of opposition. In Ireland they were still busy traders after the close of the Viking period. It is true that they might undertake raids from their new lands whenever a suitable opportunity arose, but in large measure the last quarter of the ninth century

witnessed an alteration in outlook. As the *Anglo-Saxon Chronicle* noted, 'the settlers proceeded to till the land and gain their living thereby'.

East Anglia was lucky in Guthram. Even the people of Wessex admitted that King Alfred's godson was neither an irredeemable heathen nor a ruthless tyrant. His death in 889 was recorded in the *Anglo-Saxon Chronicle* without unkindness. He was the first Viking mentioned not to attract expletives. A consequence of Guthram's statesmanship was undoubtedly the steady amalgamation of Anglian and Viking stocks in Norfolk, Suffolk, Essex, Cambridgeshire, Huntingdonshire and Bedfordshire.

Quite different was the situation in the old kingdom of Mercia, where the subjected folk were dispossessed of their land and treated as slaves. Farther north the sparseness of the indigenous population allowed concentrations of Vikings to settle down with less disturbance. Only in the old

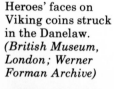

Heroes' faces on Viking coins struck in the Danelaw. *(British Museum, London; Werner Forman Archive)*

A Viking coin of the tenth century, minted in England. At least 50,000 coins were struck between 990 and 1050 from silver exacted from English subjects. *(British Museum, London; Werner Forman Archive)*

Mercian county of Lincolnshire, the flat expanse of territory adjacent to the North Sea between the Humber and the Wash, did such an arrangement happen. These thinly populated areas were planted with settlements under the leadership of Viking chieftains, the jarls who had combined together in the invading forces. Comparatively few Northumbrians had to be cleared away. The Danes living in the settlements were karls, free men under Danish law: hence the name Danelaw for their area of England. They remained loyal to the families of their original war-leaders, though the fierce struggles between rival households for supremacy may have taxed both loyalty and strength.

It is unlikely that Danelaw was coined as a name till the reign of Knut. Its introduction denoted the two systems of law and custom which then prevailed: south of Watling Street the English system, north the Danish. This does not, of course, imply uniformity within either English or Danish areas. Local customs and practices would have been observed, just as they were in other parts of Europe. But the Scandinavian origin of the system operating in the Danelaw was readily acknowledged by English law-makers. The advisers of Ethelred the Unready were aware that the Danes held legal assemblies, or things. The thing of the Five Boroughs of Lincoln, Derby, Nottingham Leicester and Stamford patently recalls the Althing of Iceland. It exercised jurisdiction over a large territory. Of seminal importance to later English law was the sworn jury used by the Danes. Twelve prominent men swore

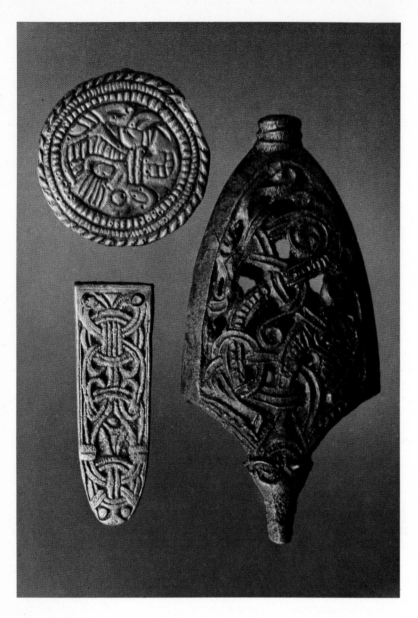

Angles, the ancestors of Alcuin. They preferred to live in the country, outside the walls of the legionary fortress, as did the Vikings on their capture of York in 867. The stubborn resistance of Saxon Wessex to Viking incursion had encouraged the invaders to switch their effort northwards. The results of civil discord in Northumbria also offered a better prospect of lasting success. Although the wrangling men of Northumberland at last united to face the Viking army at York in 867, they suffered a disastrous defeat. Ten years afterwards the conquerors had clearly put down permanent roots.

In 882 the first Christian Viking king of northern England took up residence at York. He was Guthfrith Hardaknutsson. According to Symeon of Durham, the abbot of Carlisle assisted at his coronation. The abbot had been instructed in a dream to go to the camp of the Danish army and proclaim Guthfrith king, which he did. Life in Northumbria continued to be hazardous, as Danish adventurers tried to carve out realms for themselves. In 919 the Viking dynasts of Dublin crossed the Irish Channel and retook Northumbria. Though of sterner stuff than their predecessors, they could not contain the resurgent Saxons, who at the battle of Brunanburgh in 937 seized Northumberland. 'Then the Northmen,' an unknown poet exults, 'departed in their nailed ships, bloodstained survivors of the spears.' But they came back, making England once again a maelstrom.

By 1014 the conflict had escalated into an all-time struggle between Denmark and England. The Danish king Svein Forkbeard won the whole of England that year. The war-weary people, English and Danish settlers alike, welcomed him as ruler. His son Knut, Canute the Great, strongly identified himself with England despite putting together an impressive overseas empire. It was the weakness of the Anglo-Danish line after Knut's death that exposed the country to outside attack. Neither his Danish

Decorated Viking metalwork from York, a Danish city from 867. The first Christian Viking king to live there was Guthfrith Hardaknutsson. (*Yorkshire Museum; photo: Clive Friend, FIIP, Woodmansterne Ltd.*)

on holy relics to be impartial in their dealings with suspects. Although judgement was determined by ordeal, the twelve just men had to pronounce fairly the outcome. Modern juries descend from their deliberations. Offenders against the peace were usually punished more severely under Danelaw than English writ.

The capital of the northern Danes was York, a city of note from Roman times. Parts of the massive stone walls erected by the legionaries are still visible. In the fourth century Constantine the Great had been proclaimed emperor there by the troops. After the withdrawal of the Roman legions at the beginning of the fifth century the city was taken over by the nor his English successors could protect England against renewed assault by ex-Vikings. 1066 saw the Norwegians routed at Stamford Bridge, but not the Normans at Hastings.

We term the Norman conquerors ex-Vikings for good reason. Although the descendants of Rollo's followers retained their Scandinavian vigour and strength, they developed some uncharacteristic traits during the consolidation of the dukedom of Normandy. Within three generations of the cession of 911 the language of the settlers was French and their way of living in accordance with a feudal pattern. Moreover, there were never assemblies of free men to compensate for the aristocratic bias: from the beginning Norman society was strictly hierarchical. The Norman dukes were pleased to acclaim themselves absolute rulers in the Frankish style. The conquest of England falls outside the Viking period, but the adventures of the Normans in the Mediterranean are worthy of mention. In 1016 a contingent of Norman pilgrims returning from Jerusalem was able to help the Christian princes of southern Italy against the encroaching Saracens. Salerno and Apulia were swift to call for further aid when pressed by new Muslim assaults, and a steady stream of Norman soldiers travelled south. In the confused fighting the ex-Vikings managed to establish themselves as feudal princes in southern Italy and Sicily. In 1071 Roger, son of Tancred d'Hautville, took Palermo from the Saracens and with his brother Robert went on to dominate all of Sicily. An Italian chronicler wrote in awe of Roger: 'Homer says of Achilles that those who heard his voice seemed to hear the thundering shout of a great multitude, but it is said of this man that his battle-cry would turn back tens of thousands.'

Stone cross fragments from Viking York, the seat of a Christian Danish ruler after 882. *(Yorkshire Museum; photo: Clive Friend, FIIP, Woodmansterne Ltd.)*

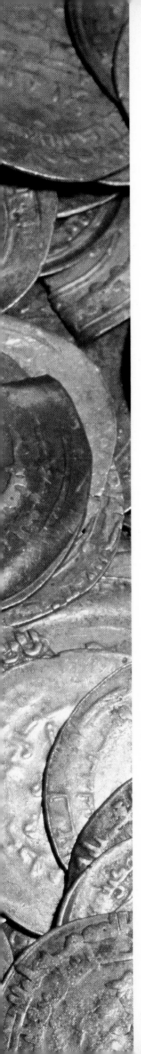

The Vikings in the East

The Vikings in the west sailed mainly from Norway and Denmark. The Swedish movement lay eastwards, across the Baltic Sea, along the great rivers of Russia, and towards the distant trading cities of Constantinople and Baghdad. The Vikings who penetrated eastwards were driven there by the same lack of challenge and opportunity at home as those pushing westward, yet their activities differed profoundly. Except for southern Finland and the lower reaches of the Volkhov river, the Swedes in the east never settled down to farming. They remained traders and raiders, the overlords of the Slav peoples within their range of attack. Ibn Rustah, an Arab writing in the first quarter of the tenth century, tells us how the Swedes busied themselves in slave-hunting as well as in the fur trade. 'They have no cultivated land,' he writes, 'but depend for their supplies on what they can get from the land of the surrounding Slavs.' Unlike the territories fought over and settled in the west, there was hardly any mingling with the native population and, once conditions stopped being favourable to the Swedes, the eastern episode disappeared almost without archaeological trace.

The Swedish Vikings were penetrating eastwards before the beginning of the ninth century. Legend insists that a swashbuckler named Ivar Vidfadmi gained control over Sweden, Denmark, Northumberland, northern Germany and the Russian lands prior to 700. He is said to have drowned on an expedition to Russia. His fabled gains are too early to merit belief. The first known attacks happened about the 850s, when the Swedes from the trading port of Birka sent forces eastwards. They exacted tribute from the inhabitants of what today is known as Latvia. Acquisitiveness marked Swedish behaviour throughout.

A precise picture of the start of the eastward movement is hard to obtain. Under what circumstances the Swedes intervened in Russian affairs we cannot tell. The *Book of Annals*, composed in Kiev around 1100, says that between 860 and 862 the peoples living in central European Russia invited a number of men to bring order to their country. Tribe fought tribe without cease and the oppressed said, 'Let us seek a prince who may rule over us and judge us according to law'. Those who came to undertake the task were 'Rus, just as some are called Swedes, others Northmen, others Angles, and others Gotlanders.' The Rus were three brothers, Rurik, Sineus and Beloozere, accompanied by their kinsfolk. 'On account of these Varangians, the district of Novgorod became known as the land of the Rus.' This is a gloss. The actual rise of Swedish influence along the Volkhov river could not have been so simple. The entry, however, is interesting as evidence of the Russian belief that the founder of the city-state of Novgorod was a prince of Scandinavian

OPPOSITE: a tenth-century hoard of Arab coins. The Vikings in Russia were traders and raiders, silver, in coin or ornament, was their particular desire. *(Museum of National Antiquities, Stockholm; Photoresources)*

61

stock. A later passage even recounts how other Rus travelled down the River Dnieper to Kiev, which they acquired 'at the same time Rurik was ruling at Novgorod'.

The word Rus appears to derive ultimately from a word meaning a rowing-way, a waterway, a road. Sweden was referred to as Ruosti by the Finns. But Rus was only used for the Swedes in Russia, never the Swedes in Sweden. Varangians has affinities to a Russian word meaning a pedlar, which in one sense the itinerant Vikings were, but some scholars consider it to be a nickname given by the Greeks. If so, it would mean something like 'the hoarse ones'. Possibly the Byzantine Greeks shared the dislike felt by Al-Tartushi for Viking singing.

The Swedes came to Russia as traders and plunderers, and they moved by two main routes, using the rivers Volga and Dnieper. The easternmost route along the Volga afforded the least scope for Viking domination. The Bulgars and the Khazars were already in firm control. The wealthy and tolerant Khazars of the lower

The river Dnieper which the Vikings used to gain access to Kiev, as a base for further exploration into the East. *(Spectrum Colour Library)*

Volga had excellent relations with the Byzantines, who appreciated their stabilizing influence on the steppes. In 834–5 engineers were dispatched from Constantinople to build a stone fortress for the Khazar king at Sarkel on the river Don. The opportunities for the Swedish migrants therefore lay primarily in the basins of the Volkhov and the Dnieper. The frontiers of the advanced states to the south, the Byzantine Empire and the Arab Caliphate of Baghdad, proved to be the limits of Viking power in that direction. Both Christian and Muslim rulers had forces strong enough to repel raids.

Archaeological evidence of the Swedish period in Russia is scarce. A characteristic riverside base would be Aldeigjuborg, as the Vikings called it, on the Volkhov about ten miles from Lake Ladoga. It possessed an earth rampart and made use of a ravine for defence. The Swedes did not found Aldeigjuborg; they joined people already living there, as at many other sites. The mixture of townsfolk is reflected in the variety of house building, though the last styles in the eleventh century are all Slavonic. A purely Viking find is a bow with a runic inscription, dating from the ninth century. Aldeigjuborg was midway between the Gulf of Finland and Novgorod, a trading station on the main rowing-way of the Rus. Settlers here probably farmed as well as traded, but the Swedes who continued upstream or crossed overland to the Volga were only adventurers and merchants. Ships and baggage, of course, had to be carried between the headwaters of the different river systems. It is reported by chroniclers that in the unsuccessful Rus assault on Constantinople in 907 ships were fitted with wheels to circumvent the Greeks, who had stretched a chain across the Bosporus. Generally we can assume that the Vikings manhandled their craft.

The Volkhov-Dnieper axis was the key to Viking power. The seizure, or

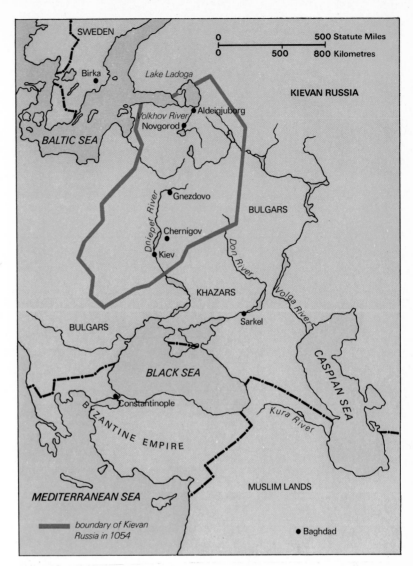

invited appropriation, of Novgorod and Kiev provided effective bases for further movement. The cemetry at Grezdovo, later Smolensk, has yielded articles of Scandinavian origin. This settlement was sited on the Dnieper at the transfer-point for craft from the Volkhov. The remains indicate the presence of Vikings down the length of the axis. Novgorod itself is largely unexcavated, but we know from runic inscriptions in Scandinavia that there was a church there dedicated to St Olaf, the Norwegian monarch famed for his peacemaking and his good laws. From Kiev, where the Dnieper is half a mile wide, merchants would float downstream to the Black Sea, and then to Constantinople. Hostile Khazar tribesmen as well as rapids made the journey a dangerous one. On reaching the delta of the Dnieper,

Statue of St Olaf, royal patron saint of Norway, to whom a church was dedicated by the Vikings at Novgorod. *(Statens Historiska Museet, Stockholm; Werner Forman Archive*

and with it the safety of the open sea, it was customary for the Swedes to sacrifice to their gods. Ibn Fadlan, an Arab trader, witnessed one of these celebrations of safe passage on the Volga. He says that the Vikings moored their ships and took ashore bread, meat, onions, milk and beer as offerings to deities carved on wooden poles. Each Rus informed the god of his goods and his hopes, beseeching divine aid in encountering a rich buyer.

Kiev is referred to as 'the capital of the Varangians' in the *Book of Annals*. It was raised to the status of 'mother of Russian cities' by Oleg, Rurik's successor at Novgorod and conqueror of Kiev in 880–2. After winning the southern capital, we are told, he 'began to build stockaded towns, and imposed tribute on the Slavs' and other peoples. By 907 Oleg considered himself strong enough to move against Constantinople itself. Two thousand vessels are supposed to have conveyed eighty thousand men to assault the city. Whatever the numbers, they were inadequate for the task. The fortifications of Constantinople were the wonder of Europe and they were

breached only once, in 1453. Moreover, the population of the city must have numbered half a million, a concentration beyond Viking experience and belief.

Oleg's raid should perhaps be viewed as a development of the piracy that the Swedes had commenced on the Black Sea in the 860s. Its result was the Rus-Byzantine commercial treaty of 911–12, which turned the Byzantine Empire into Kiev's chief trading partner. The peace lasted for a generation, then in 941 a prince Igor arrived with a fleet. Though repulsed by Greek fire, he returned three years later to the attack. A compromise was reached whereby the Rus were given permission to ravage Bulgaria and, in the new commercial treaty of 945, they were granted certain trading rights at Constantinople. Rus could purchase silk, enter the city unarmed and in small numbers, and stay in the neighbourhood during the spring and summer months. But no permanent trading post was permitted. This wise policy of the Greeks tamed Viking greed just as the diversion of Viking ferocity against the Bulgars, rather than the

The walls of Constantinople which proved their strength as fortifications against Oleg's men in 907. *(Spectrum Colour Library)*

65

Arab metalwork from a Swedish grave. The Viking raid of 943 along the Kura river was intended to plunder pieces such as these amulets and coins. (*Museum of National Antiquities, Stockholm; Photoresources*)

Khazars, left the balance of power in southern Russia undisturbed.

The Rus also traded and raided in Muslim territories. 912 saw a foray on the Caspian. In 943 a fleet entered the Kura River and laid waste an extensive area in what is today Russian Azerbaijan. Yet the Viking victory was hollow, for Muslim reinforcements cut off the line of retreat and the Rus had to extricate themselves slowly and painfully. Muslim arms and dysentery took their toll of the raiders. By necessity, the usual relationship between the Rus and Baghdad was peaceful trade.

Commercial contact with the Greeks was always stronger. Kievan Russia via the Black Sea was a natural hinterland for Constantinople. Vladimir, a Swede by descent in spite of the un-Norse name, created a far-flung empire during his reign (980–1015). He claimed suzerainty over the majority of the Slavic peoples. With a professional army recruited in Sweden, Vladimir defeated the Poles and twice beat the Bulgars. In order to safeguard his territories from nomad attack he built several lines of forts along the northern banks of the steppe rivers. These fortifications became the model for generations of Russian rulers. Immigrant peoples were granted lands around the fortresses, which acted as rallying points for their resistance in times of incursion. But the leadership of outlying portions of the state was kept in the hands of Vladimir's sons or faithful adherents.

The structure of Kievan Russia was subjected to great strain towards the close of Vladimir's reign by the revolt of his ablest son Yaroslav, who was viceroy of Novgorod. Yaroslav refused to send revenues to Kiev in 1014; two-thirds of the annual taxes were remitted to the central treasury, the remaining third being expended locally. Vladimir died making preparations against Novgorod and a complicated struggle between his sons ensued. Their bitter animosity may be explained partly by the fact that they were not all of the same mother. Vladimir's chosen heir was Boris, one of the youngest sons, so the withholding of revenues by Yaroslav can be interpreted as a calculated gamble for the throne. It would have been easy for his agents to travel the short distance from Novgorod to Sweden and raise contingents of soldiers there with the money. In the event, Yaroslav was obliged to share power with his brother Mstislav till 1036. Yaroslav ruled from Novgorod, Mstislav from Chernigov, Kiev ceasing to be the capital in these years.

Vladimir himself was the Rus equivalent of the Danish Svein Forkbeard, an ambitious king who drew his military strength for distant conquest from the surplus population of Scandinavia. His schemes were financed by expanding trade. During the winter months his officials would tour the Slavic peoples subject to tribute and bring back to Kiev furs, wax, honey and slaves. Some tribes paid in coin. Simultaneously, the Slavs living on the Dnieper were charged with the manufacture of craft for the spring voyage downstream. Fitted out and loaded at Kiev in May each year, the armada was sent to the markets of Byzantium in the south.

In 988 Vladimir had acknowledged the Christian Church and Greek Orthodox missionaries entered Russia. We are told that he toyed with Judaism, Islam and Christianity before accepting the latter faith. His envoys in Constantinople were especially impressed with St Sophia, the most magnificent cathedral in Christendom. After attending a service amid its sparkling mosaics, they turned and said to their hosts: 'We knew not whether we were in heaven or on Earth.' On the terrestrial plane, the newly converted Vladimir could be of immediate comfort to the young Byzantine emperor Basil II (976–1025), then harassed by the Bulgars in Europe and by aristocratic rebels in Asia Minor. Six thousand Rus were ordered to Constantinople. With the aid of these soldiers the imperial army managed to win the day. The price Basil had to pay, after a display of reluctance and military prodding from Vladimir, was the marriage of his sister to the Kievan ruler and virtual autonomy for the Russian Church.

The depth of Vladimir's own belief is obscure. We know he avidly col-

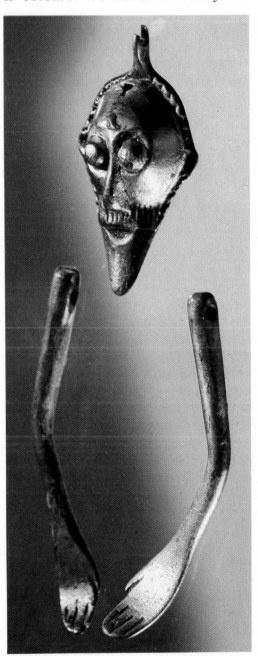

Silver pendant of a Viking, from the trading mart of Birka in Swedish Uppland. Birka's commercial activity was dependent on the Russian connection. *(Statens Historiska Museet, Stockholm; Werner Forman Archive)*

lected relics of the saints, sacred vessels and icons. Recorded in the *Book of Annals* too is his lavish charity. 'He invited', an entry informs us, 'each beggar and poor man to come to the palace and receive whatever he needed, both food and drink, and money from the treasury.' For those who were too ill or weak to come themselves, he ordered wagons to deliver 'bread, fish, various vegetables, mead in casks, and rye-beer'. The maintenance of churches was provided for by means of a tithe, levied on princes, merchants and landlords. The introduction of Christianity was Vladimir's most momentous decision. The Kievan state, weakened by perpetual hostilities with its nomadic neighbours, broke into warring principalities after 1054. But the Orthodox Church stayed on and, by Vladimir's own stipulation, the language adopted for its services was Slavonic. The Viking era in Russia had passed.

What was the contribution of the Swedes to Russia? Opinion is divided. One school of thought would see the foundation of the Kievan state as fundamental. The Vikings are credited with the establishment of the cities of European Russia and hence the pillars of the Russian state. Another school argues that the Viking intervention was a passing phase in the development of Russia, the Slavs alone being responsible for its formation. The sparsity of historical and archaeological data enhances the dispute. The truth probably lies somewhere between the two propositions. Taking over existing settlements along the chief waterways of central European Russia, the Vikings stimulated commercial enterprise and by feat of arms added to their importance. They drew together Slavic peoples and brought them into a mutually beneficial relationship with the Byzantine Empire.

The accomplishments of the last Kievan King provide a fine example of the Viking contribution. Yaroslav, the rebellious son of Vladimir, brought his country on to the stage of European politics. Kievan Russia was accepted as a member of Christendom. Its wealth allowed the building of city walls, palaces, cathedrals, churches and fine houses. Furthermore, it paid for the translation of books into the Slavonic tongue. Though Yaroslav was foolishly tempted to raid Constantinople in 1043, a lapse costly in men and materials, the Kievan frontiers were open to a civilizing influence from the Byzantine Greeks.

Kievan Russia indicates how far the wild Vikings had come. Their initial uncouthness was legendary. In 922 Ibn Fadlan could wonder at their forthright behaviour and he was taken aback by the sexual habits of the adventurers he met. We hear of the quarrelsomeness and violence of Rus settlements, the frequent recourse to single combat as well as the seemingly interminable blood-feuds. There was also the custom of sacrifice to the gods by hanging. Death was sudden and men carried weapons at all times. Against an external enemy the Rus would fight as one man, but remove that threat and each warrior must see to his own security. Most horrible of all was the burying of favourite women in the grave mounds of Rus chieftains.

Finally, a word is needed on the Swedes who served the Greek emperors as soldiers. Many adventurers gave up raiding for service in the imperial armies. Around 1000 the Varangians were organized as the emperor's personal guard. In 1034 Harald the Ruthless, who was slain at Stamford Bridge in 1066, enlisted with a personal following of five hundred men. He fought in campaigns the length and breadth of the empire before returning to Scandinavia in 1042. The Varangian guard was a crack force, thrown into the thick of the fighting: it suited the axe-wielding men from the cold north. But after the Norman Conquest its composition was no longer exclusively Varangian. Discontented Saxons and Danes from England came to swell the ranks.

OPPOSITE: a runic memorial in Sweden. Stones like this one were raised to warriors who died at home or abroad in Russia and Byzantium. *(Photoresources)*

68

Viking Mythology

No survey of the Vikings would be complete without an understanding of the religious beliefs that occupied the thoughts and emotions of the early Viking raiders. It was only during the early eleventh century that the Vikings were finally persuaded to the Christian faith. Up until then, a host of pagan gods inspired the minds of raider, soldier, trader and farmer alike. To ascertain the original Viking mind we have to look at traditional conceptions about the gods and men. We find ourselves turning inevitably to the old religious beliefs expressed in the highly developed Norse myths.

Viking mythology was complex and vast. Its pantheon found space for a variety of rumbustious deities, some of whom were patently late arrivals on the cosmic scene. The Vikings called their gods *aesir*. Snorri Sturluson (1179–1241) thought that the word derived from the word Asia, making Thor a grandson of Priam of Troy and Odin his descendant in the twentieth generation. Although this derivation seems unlikely, it is quite possible that a second group of deities, the *vanir*, were translated from Asia Minor at a late date. The vanir are said to have originally lived on the Don river, 'formerly called Vanaquisl'. The two groups warred against each other, till they realized that neither could score a final triumph and an agreement was reached. Odin was accepted as chief of the aesir, while the goddess Freya took a leading role among the vanir.

Pitted against the gods was a race of frost giants, the descendants of Bergelmir. The father of the frost giants was Ymir, who arose from the icy waves. He was evil and associated with the numbing cold, which Vikings sailing in Arctic waters knew only too well. Odin, Vili and Ve – the sons of Bor – fought and slew Ymir, so much blood pouring from his gaping wounds that the remaining frost giants, with the exception of Bergelmir and his wife, were drowned. The sons of Bor took Ymir's carcass to Ginnungagap, the primordial abyss, and made the soil from his flesh, the mountain crags from his bones, and boulders from his toes. Out of the excess of blood they formed the lakes and seas. Maggot-like within the carcass of Ymir, innumerable dwarfs grew up, and at the word of the gods they acquired human intelligence and shape. Their dwelling-places were inside caves and holes in the ground. Ymir's skull was made into heaven, held up by four dwarfs, and the giant's brains, flung into the winds, became the clouds.

Having ordered earth and the heavens in this fashion, the sons of Bor went on to create man. Discovering on the sea-shore two logs of driftwood, they picked them up and whittled them into mankind. Each of the brothers gave mankind certain gifts: Odin gave 'the precious soul'; Vili, understanding and the emotions; and Vi, senses and form. It is a myth that relates to Odin as a wind god, a leader of souls rushing through the air.

LEFT: a hog back Viking tomb from Heysham in England. It shows the four dwarfs set by Odin to support the heavens. (*Werner Forman Archive*)

An entry of 1127 in the *Old English Chronicle* tells how one night many people watched huntsmen in the sky. They 'were black, huge, and hideous, and rode on black horses and on black he-goats, and their hounds were jet black, with eyes like saucers, and horrible. This was seen in the deer park of the town of Peterborough, and in all the woods that stretch from that town to Stamford, and all through the night the monks heard them sounding and winding their horns.' Even after conversion to Christianity and the Norman conquest, it would seem that the furious host of Odin Atridir, 'the rider', continued to haunt the skies above the old Danelaw.

The genesis of the sons of Bor is explained in a bovine myth. According to this story, the primeval cow Audumla, or nourisher, licked the icy rocks which were salty to her taste. By the evening of the first day there appeared from the ice, at the spot where she was licking, the hair of a man; on the second day, a man's head; on the third day, an entire man. This was Buri, 'the born one', handsome, tall and strong. He begat a son called Bor who took to wife Bestla, the daughter of a frost giant: their sons were Odin, Vili and Ve.

Odin was the god most favoured by the Vikings. From Snorri Sturluson we gather that Odin rose in esteem during the eighth and ninth centuries, taking over many of the functions of the sky god. 'He had his way in all things. Mighty as the other gods may be, yet they all serve him as children do their father.' Odin was father of the gods, father of the slain, and lord of men. 'Shifty-eyed and flaming-eyed', he oversaw cargoes, granted wishes as well as victories, and was known for his wide wisdom and swift deceit. At some stage Odin must have displaced Tyr, known to the Romans as the ancient sky god of the northern

The chief son of Bor, Odin. The statue comes from Skane, a Danish possession in the Viking era. *(Statens Historiska Museet, Stockholm; Werner Forman Archive)*

lands, and through this elevation restricted his rival Thor to the role of a thunder god. Tyr was an old synonym for 'god', and the chief myth by which the deposed god was remembered shows him as guardian of the sky. When he stopped the wolf Fenrir from devouring the sun and moon, his hand was bitten off by the wolf's jaws. While Tyr adjusted to a lesser authority over the fray – warriors called upon him in their prayers as a battle commenced – Odin and his two brothers, Vili and Ve were raised to the rank of creator deities. Odin, the Allfather, existed 'from the beginning of time', creating 'heaven and earth and sky and all within them', and ruling 'with immense power'.

The Romans identified Odin with Mercury. They regarded him as a psychopomp, a leader of souls. To Odin were dedicated the slain, both men and horses. Sometimes an oath was sworn to send all the vanquished to the god's care; as an act of dedication, an enemy might be cut down on the spot, or prisoners hanged, naked or clothed, from trees. The devastation of the earliest Viking attacks can be seen as part of his worship. The slaughter at Nantes in 842 was probably the fulfilment of such a barbarous pledge. Ibn Fadlan tells us that in 922 it was commonplace to seek divine favour on certain days with human victims and he noticed the use of hanging in the sacrifices of the Rus.

Hanging was inextricably bound up with Odin worship. A myth celebrates the god's own experience of the

Tyr, the old sky god of the North. He is shown trying to bind the Fenrir wolf, which bit off his hand. The matrice was probably used in the manufacture of helmet plaques. *(Statens Historiska Museet, Stockholm; Werner Forman Archive*

gallows, when he hung himself on the world ash, Yggdrasill, in order to learn the secret of the runes of wisdom. Yggdrasill was called 'the horse of wood', or 'Odin's mount'. The cosmic tree was thought to hold the universe together, its branches overhanging the 'nine worlds' – those of the aesir, the vanir, the light elves, the dark elves, men, the giants, the dwarfs, the dead, and the fiery southlands. It had three mighty roots: one reached down to the land of the frost giants, where stood the wisdom-well of Mimir; the second ended in foggy Niflheim, where from below Nidhoggr, a dreadful beast, gnawed at the root; the last embedded itself in Asgard, the stronghold of the gods, and beneath it was the sacred well of Urdr, where divine judgement took place. A continuous tussle was in progress between the forces of destruction and the forces of reconstruction within Yggdrasill. From Urdr magic clay and water was always needed to repair damage, whether the stripping away of leaves, rotting bark, or fractured roots. The Vikings believed that when decay outran renewal the tree would shudder, shaking the universe and signalling doomsday.

Odin's sacrifice to himself, as the Vikings referred to his hanging, resulted in Yggdrasill being looked upon as a Tree of Knowledge. The wisdom he won from the nine-day ordeal may have been thought to have come ultimately from the mysterious wells of Mimir and Urdr. One legend says that Odin threw one of his eyes into the well of Mimir, a renowned sage, the sacrifice gaining

Yggdrasill. The carved relief on the Urnes stave church, western Norway. *(Werner Forman Archive)*

him untold knowledge. Another legend says he received Mimir's severed head, which he preserved with herbs and magic spells. The idea of a speaking head also occurs in Celtic mythology. Less accessible to Odin would have been the secrets of Urdr, the three giant maidens who brought Time into the universe. Their names were Past, Present and Future; collectively, the three sisters were known as the Nornir, or the Fates, to whom Odin and the gods owed obedience. The Anglo-Saxons in Britain called Urdr by the name of Wyrd, which meant destiny, and they maintained their belief in the tremendous authority of these three sisters long after the coming of Christianity. The Weird Sisters in Shakespeare's *Macbeth* clearly owe something to the Nornir.

A method employed by Odin to keep watch on events is reminiscent of Viking practice at sea. Just as the long boats sent out ravens in search of land, so Odin had two ravens that would 'whisper into his ears every scrap of news which they saw or heard tell of'. Every morning these faithful birds flew round the 'nine worlds'. Yet Odin was often tempted to go and look for himself, usually wandering from place to place as an old man – one-eyed, grey-bearded and wearing a floppy-brimmed hat.

The influence of the Odin cult was felt most strongly on the battlefield. There the gallows god was transformed into a ferocious, savage and cruel spiller of blood. His wolves and ravens welcomed the dead. As father of the slain, Odin gathered to Valhalla all brave men who died in battle. Those fated to fall were touched by Valkyries, Odin's handmaidens. Once domiciled at Valhalla, the hall of the slain in Asgard, the happy dead were trained into the finest army ever seen in the universe. Each day they fought together in the meadows outside Valhalla, then as the night approached they went inside the great hall to feast on pork and down vast

quantities of mead, taking their brimming cups from the hands of the Valkyries. Odin himself ate not a crumb; wine was to him both food and drink. This existence must have seemed ideal to the hardy Viking – better to lose one's life in the thick of the fight and become one of Odin's sons than die of sickness or age and travel northwards to Hel, the cold and wet land of the dead. With this kind of choice, it is not surprising that the raider and soldier from Scandinavia threw himself straight into a fight. It helps to explain the military impact of the longships, the devastating punch delivered by their small crews.

Odin recruited his army of dead heroes to forearm himself against the predicted decline of the gods, the 'axe-age, sword-age, storm-age, wolf-age, before the earth is overthrown'. He had learned of the final defeat and doom of the gods, the ragnarok, through the wisdom acquired on Yggdrasill. The conflict would take place upon the Vigrid plain. This notion attracted the Vikings, being a

Odin with his two whispering ravens, as depicted on a gold bracteate from a Norwegian hoard. *(University Historical Museum, Oslo; Photoresources)*

parallel of their own troubled time. They would have seen themselves as sailing into the very jaws of annihilation, just like the gods. The foolhardy assaults on Seville, Rome and Constantinople were simply a testing of destiny, a provocation of the Nornir. Just as the cycle of Norse myth started with a world awash with Ymir's blood, so the last scene was a battlefield where the gods were predestined to gush out their own blood.

Ragnarok would commence with the death of Balder, Odin's second son, and the realization by the gods that, in the sly Loki, the fire giant and the murderer, they had tolerated the growth of evil. 'The bleeding god', Balder, may be a northern derivative of the dying-and-rising deities of West Asia. It was said that the return of Balder would happen in the new world, the green land risen from the sea, after the destruction of the gods. The legends say that Balder would be killed by a shaft of mistletoe, always considered in Europe to be a mysterious and sacred plant. Hodr was the blind god who, used as a catspaw by Loki, flung the deadly shaft. When Balder fell, Asgard was thrown into

confusion, till Frigg suggested that someone ride to Hel so as to find out the ransom desired. This dark world, rain-swept and wretchedly cold, was the place of the dead who would fight against the gods upon the Vigrid plain. Its queen, also named Hel, was the monstrous offspring of Loki. She looked as a rotting corpse, putrid and foul; her palace was Sleetcold, the seat from which she tyrannized those who had died of disease, old age or unheroic accident. Balder was known as the 'god of tears' because his brother, Hermodr, rode back on Sleipnir, the eight-legged stallion of Odin, with the message that the condition of release from Hel was that all created things should weep for him – as they did, all except Loki, whom the gods chained for his impudence.

Yet Asgard knew it was too late. The end was upon the gods. The wolf Fenrir gobbled up the sun and bit a lump out of the moon; the sea serpent Jormungandr boiled up the deep, blowing clouds of poison over the earth and sky; and the Naglfar, the ghastly ship made from the nail parings of those buried unshorn, broke her moorings down in Hel. On the

OPPOSITE: a carved funerary stone from Gotland, eigth century. Notice on the right, Odin's eight-legged stallion Sleipnir. *(Statens Historiska Museet, Stockholm; Werner Forman Archive)*

BELOW: horses fighting. The god Odin was usually associated with stallions so that this sport may have been part of his worship. A fifth century carving on stone from Sweden. *(Museum of National Antiquities, Stockholm; Photoresources)*

Vigrid plain the forces of evil were mustered – Fenrir and Jormungandr along with Loki and Hrymr who led the frost giants – and against them marched the gods and the slain sons of Odin, in full knowledge of their impending doom. As Yggdrasill shook the fight began. In the rout fell Odin, Thor, Tyr, the wolf Fenrir, and the sea serpent as well as myriad combatants, till at last Surtr, the 'black' fire giant form of Loki, pitched flames over the earth and turned heaven to cinders. The cosmic scene is one of desolation, where the sun has darkened, stars have crashed from the sky, and the sea has submerged the land.

After Odin, the most important god was the boisterous Thor, often called 'Whip-it-up Thor'. He was chiefly a thunder god, whose devotees were the farmers and traders. Thor did not possess the quicksilver intelligence of Odin, nor his incalculable power over the living and the dead. He was mocked for his slow wit and the way frost giants constantly made a fool out of him. Yet his failings – the enormous hunger and thirst that possessed him, the straightforwardness that aided his enemies, and the boundless energy that got him into so many scrapes – endeared him to generations of the Scandinavian peoples. We are assured by Adam of Bremen in 1200 that Thor was the mightiest deity of Uppsala. Thor was above all the protector, the scourge of the frost giants, who represented the forces of the cold northern lands working against man.

The most famous journey to Giantland was the occasion that Loki accompanied Thor, and they encountered Vasty, a frost giant so enormous that the gods inadvertently slept in the thumb of his empty glove, thinking it was a room. When Thor increased his own size with his magic belt and attempted to smash the skull of the sleeping giant with his thunder hammer, Vasty awoke in the belief that either a leaf or a twig had brushed his brow. Afterwards they reached the city of Outguard, whose battlements were so high that they could not see their summit. Inside this strange city Thor and his companion failed in a number of contests, the thunder god himself being wrestled down on one knee by 'an old, old woman'. Only on the journey home did the disconcerted pair of gods appreciate that Vasty and Outguard were illusions, stupendous magical creations sent out by the timorous giants to baffle mighty Thor.

One legend tells of the time when Thor and the frost giant Hymir went fishing together for the sea serpent Jormungandr. A colossal hook baited with the head of a huge ox caught in the monster's throat, and Thor would have landed the prize had not the sight of Jormungandr rising from the depths of the sea terrified Hymir. In panic the giant cut the line and then dived overboard – to escape the anger of the frustrated fisherman. Another who annoyed Thor was the stone giant Hrungnir, clearly a personification of the icy mountain peaks. The gods asked him to fight Hrungnir because of the nuisance he was causing Odin. In single combat Thor felled the giant with his hammer, but sustained an injury himself, a piece of stone having lodged in his head.

A much enjoyed legend concerns the stealing of Thor's potent weapon. The *Thrymskirda*, dating from about 900, tells how the frost giants secreted the hammer. Loki brought news of its hiding place and persuaded Thor into a cunning trick for its recovery. The frost giant King Thrymr had demanded the hand of the goddess Freya in exchange for the hammer, so Loki suggested that Thor travel to Giantland disguised as Freya with himself pre-

Thor, the thunder god. He was a favourite deity of farmers, like the Viking settlers in Iceland who worshipped this statue. *(Werner Forman Archive)*

tending to be a maidservant. Dressed in women's clothing, the two gods arrived for the wedding. At the nuptial feast Thrymr was astonished to see the bride eat a whole ox, eight salmon and all the dainties intended for the ladies, washing them down with three barrels of wine. Cunning Loki explained away the singular appetite by saying that the bride had been too excited to eat or drink for a week before the marriage. When Thrymr took out the hammer, Thor grasped it and laid low all the giants in attendance. Such a sudden burst of violence would not have been unknown at a Viking feast.

Odin and Thor were of the aesir, Freya of the vanir. The brother of Freya was Frey, a fertility god, the son of the sea god Njord. Snorri Sturluson comments on Frey's appearance, saying he was 'the most beautiful of the gods, having power over the rain and sunshine together with the natural increase of the earth.' He directed the good fortunes of men as the giver of fruitful seasons and peace. His cult had orgiastic rituals and the ritual copulation at the time of a chieftain's burial certainly reflects the worship of Frey. Ibn Fadlan watched a complete ceremony in 922 on the Volga river. He says that a female slave of the dead chieftain elected to join him in the grave, which she did after a period of merriment and mating with the leading men of the community. She was strangled on the bed where the body of the chieftain reposed and a flaming torch was applied to the ship in which the deathbed stood. After the ship, the chieftain, and the girl were reduced to ashes, a mound was built over the place. On inquiry Ibn Fadlan was informed that whereas interment let worms devour the

RIGHT: phallic Frey, the Norse god of generation. Bronze statue from Sweden. *(Statens Historiska Museet, Stockholm; Werner Forman Archive)*

LEFT: Freya, the goddess demanded by the frost giant king Thrymr in exchange for Thor's stolen hammer. *(Statens Historiska Museet, Stockholm; Werner Forman Archive)*

body, and was an indignity not to be imposed on an honoured Viking, fire destroyed in a moment, wafting away the spirit to the land beyond. The finest vessel ever launched was the ship belonging to Frey. Known as Skidbladnir, this craft had a favourable wind as soon as the sail was hoisted and yet, the voyage done, Frey was able to fold everything away into his trouser pocket.

The mischief maker of Norse mythology was Loki. Fickle and false, clever and cunning, the trickster god Loki was 'the father of lies'. Probably a personification of the forest fire, one of the most destructive agents known to the Vikings, he was instrumental in causing the downfall of the gods. Like fire, he was a good servant and a bad master. On one hand he assisted Thor on his various adventures in Giantland and he presented Frey with Skidbladnir. On the other hand, he brought down Balder with the mistletoe and helped to overwhelm the gods on the Vigrid plain. This evil tendency in Loki indicates his kinship with the wild, untamed forces of the universe. He could erupt with the deadly fire of one of the Icelandic volcanoes. Moreover, Loki sired the Fenrir wolf, the sea serpent Jormungandr, and lastly Hel. Although Odin assigned duties to this progeny, he was aware of the ultimate disaster they would wreak. They were 'Odin's bane'. The Vikings feared their manifestation in wolves, sea beasts and unheroic death. The men of the longships always felt an affinity with the trials of the hardpressed gods themselves. Ragnarok beckoned the world, at least till Christianity brought a less violent faith to the Vikings.

A Swedish Viking's grave of about 850. The stones form the outline of a ship, perhaps recalling Frey's miraculous craft, Skidbladnir. (*Werner Forman Archive*)

Viking Arts and Crafts

Viking art, like Viking religion, resisted continental European influence for most of the period 750–1050. Although its decorative style had descended from Germanic forms prior to the fourth century, Scandinavian artists and craftsmen steadily developed along their own distinctive lines. They were untouched by the revival of classical precepts under Charlemagne and the Romanesque style so popular in southern lands. Their anti-classicism stayed strong and during the flood of Viking conquest expressed itself confidently in animal ornament and abstract design. Absent from surviving examples are plant motifs: an unbroken devotion to animals as a source of inspiration is a characteristic of Viking art.

Another feature common to Viking religion and art is homogeneity. An unwillingness to ape slavishly contemporary European or West Asian models meant that artists and craftsment working at great distances from each other did not diverge significantly in their approach. It is true that raiders and traders brought back with them a variety of beautiful objects, many of which we know profoundly impressed the Vikings, but the adaptation of these pieces in a brooch or a sword-handle should be seen as an incorporation within a flourishing native tradition. It is a sad fact that many works in gold and silver were melted down to provide the artist with raw materials. Yet this action, however regretful in terms of the artistic heritage of the world, exactly underlines the purposes of Viking artists and craftsmen. Their skills were employed to decorate articles of daily use: their tortuous designs appeared on helmets, shields, swords, brooches, pendants, drinking vessels, the stems and sterns of ships and memorial stones. Viking art was essentially applied art.

Several artistic styles have been identified. A seminal one was the Borre style, named from the town of Borre, near Oseberg in southern Norway. It exhibits three distinct motifs. First, there is the so-called gripping beast, a fantastic animal gripping with its paws either another beast or itself. Secondly, a leonine creature appears, with a backward-looking head. The last motif comprises an interlacing pattern of cords, straps or chains. Examples of Borre style occur on stone monuments in the Danelaw and the Isle of Man.

There are numerous gripping beasts carved on the famous Oseberg ship. This small royal craft, which plied in coastal waters, was in its old age used for the burial of a Norwegian queen, possibly at the close of the ninth century. The interment took place in ground that preserved the ship and its cargo of offerings, a wagon, three sledges, and many domestic articles. Today it stands restored in the Viking Ships Museum at Oslo. The visitor cannot but marvel at the exuberance of the decoration. He is confronted with vigorous carvings of gripping beasts, biting birds and writhing snakes. The gripping beast in its many transformations fascinated and intrigued Viking artists and craftsmen.

This ninth-century silver cup, partly gilded and inlaid with niello, beautifully demonstrates the Vikings' use of animals in their crafts. *(Michael Holford Library)*

This silver hilt of a
sword shows the
lavish decoration
used by craftsmen
in adorning articles
of daily use.
*(Michael Holford
Library)*

Rather paradoxically, the most splendid representation is found in the north portal of the stave church of Urnes, a tiny village in western Norway. It is the apotheosis of Scandinavian carving. Everything is elongated and refined, so that the labyrinthine forms of animal and serpent are marvellously entangled with the leaves of plants.

Quite aside from this tradition are the Gotland picture-stones. Many hundreds of sandstone and limestone monuments exist on the island, and those dating from the Viking period have scenes depicting both daily life and mythical events. The bas-reliefs show voyages, battles, feasts, and the

One of the many vigorous carvings to be seen on the sledges in the Oseberg ship burial. *(Viking Ships Museum, Oslo; Photoresources)*

welcome accorded slain heroes at Valhalla. It was the custom in the eighth and ninth centuries to erect these stones, which often reach 12 feet (4 metres) in height. The runestones placed at Jelling by Harald Bluetooth, the Danish king, were carved in accordance with the animal style of decoration. In all cases the inscribers and carvers on stone seem not to have used a chisel but a pointed hammer, similar to the ice-axe of the modern climber.

Improvements in the use of metals made the clearing of forests easier. The new tools were of importance to the farmer, but so were weapons. In the fields it was dangerous to stray too far from one's sword and shield. Weaponry gave the Vikings an opportunity for impressive decoration. A waist-high, double-bladed sword found in Northumberland has five bands of silver on its handle. A great iron axe-head unearthed at Mammen in Jutland is finely inlaid with silver. On one of its faces writhes a beast, part lion, part bird. Archaeologists have also recovered spearheads with decorated silver hilts. From Vendel in Swedish Uppland they have dug helmets, weapons, and metal plates for belts as well as harnesses. Particularly striking is a seventh-century helmet in iron and bronze. The cap is of iron and a bronze crest runs down the centre to a projecting nose-guard. Decoration includes curling beasts directly above the eyes and two faces, one human and the other not, on the nose-guard and the front of the crest. Other helmets have been discovered in the Vendel cemetery: they were put in the graves not later than the eighth century.

The smith's achievement during the Viking era was considerable. He was technically accomplished and fully capable of following the intricacies of his brother craftsmen, the wood-carver and the stonemason. He could work efficiently and elegantly in iron and bronze; he could inlay delicately with silver as well as hammer and

engrave the metal; and he could cast jewellery in silver and gold.

The overlap between the religion of the Norse gods and the Christian faith is illustrated in a Scandinavian mould belonging to a goldsmith. The enterprising craftsmen prepared a mould that would simultaneously produce Christian and pagan amulets. Thor's

The Mammen axe-head. *(National Museum of Copenhagen; Werner Forman Archive)*

OPPOSITE: detail from a Gotland picture stone, showing a scene from Valhalla. *(Michael Holford)*

LEFT: a silver arm ring of the tenth century. *(National Museum, Copenhagen; Werner Forman Archive)*

BELOW: two silver rings, showing the considerable achievements of the Viking silversmiths. *(Michael Holford Library)*

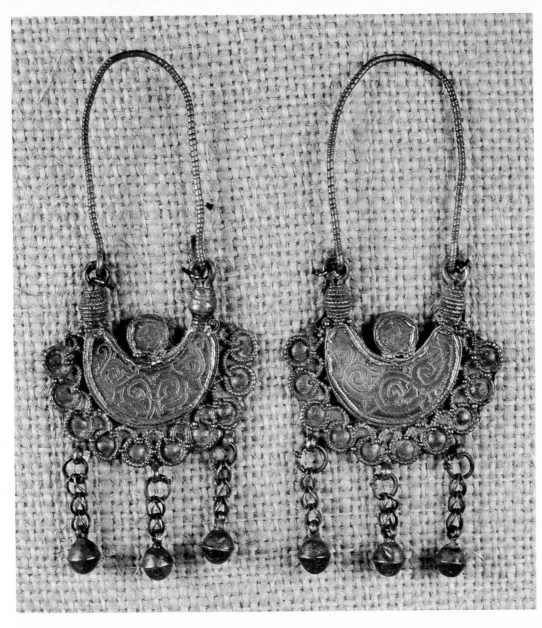

A pair of tenth-century silver earrings from Torsta in Sweden. *(Michael Holford Library)*

hammer was cast side by side with the Cross. For sheer accomplishment in jewellery-making the filigree brooch from the Danish cemetery of Lindholm Høje is remarkable. This eleventh- or early twelfth-century piece takes the form of an animal in the elongated style of the Urnes wood-carvings. The assymetrical lines of the beast and the surrounding tendrils are especially pleasing, and the brooch displays an extravagance normally associated with baroque art. The Vikings loved ornament for its own sake.

This pleasure in ornamentation is equally evident on what must surely be the fullest artistic expression of the Viking age, namely the longship. The peculiar perfection of Viking craft seems to raise them to a level higher than utility. Not for nothing has the longship become the enduring symbol of the Vikings. The ship was one of the signs portrayed in Bronze Age rock-carvings. And the vessel with 'a prow at each end' was familiar to the Romans. Skill with boats and ships descended from ancient times in Scandinavia. The coastal waters – the islands, fjords, rivers, lakes and seas – drew the men of the cold north to navigation and, as we have seen, turned them into pre-eminent sailors and explorers. The Vikings advance overseas would not have appeared as an onslaught if the raiders of the

eighth and ninth centuries had not been so incredibly mobile. Their speed, of course, depended entirely on their boats.

The building of fast vessels was stimulated through the internecine conflicts of Scandinavia. The swiftness of a shore raid determined its success and a tardy withdrawal meant not only having to deal with a counter-attack but also the chance that the loot might be forfeited. The strand-hogg, the coastal strike, was the breeding ground of the sleek longship, which attained its mature form in the

eighth century. The Oseberg ship was not a true longship, its function being a royal barge. The vessel excavated at nearby Gokstad, however, was with-out question a warship. Long and lean, the Gokstad ship measures nearly 80 feet (24.4 metres) from stem to stern, 17 feet (5.3 metres) in the beam and, fully laden, has a draught of only about 3 feet (1 metre). The keel, just over 57 feet (17 metres) long, is cut from a single oak log. The planks, averaging 1 inch (2.5 centimetres) in thickness, are fixed together with iron rivets driven through from the outside and secured inside by means of small iron plates. Nineteen cross-beams give shape to the hull and a removable deck allows space for storage.

The seaworthiness of the Gokstad longship for ocean crossings was demonstrated in 1893 when an exact replica sailed from Norway to Newfoundland through stormy seas in twenty-eight days. The captain, Magnus Anderson, recalled that they 'often had the pleasure of darting through the water at speeds of 10, and sometimes even 11 knots! This in spite of a primitive and relatively simple rigging'. Though the gunwale twisted out of true by six inches during the voyage, the vessel suffered no leaks at all. Apart from this remarkable buoyancy and elasticity in the face of the Atlantic rollers – a capacity to ride out bad weather that many a Viking must have thanked Thor and Odin for – the very shallow draught would have been a real asset. The longship could penetrate the smallest rivers, approach shelving beaches, and disembark men close to the point of attack.

The Gokstad ship was constructed with oak, except for the planking of the deck and the oars. These were pine. The means of propulsion consisted of sixteen pairs of oars as well as a big square sail made of heavy woollen cloth strengthened with rope. The mast itself was about 35 feet (10.7 metres) tall, and the yard some 37 feet (11.3 metres) long. Steering was achieved by a side-rudder fastened to the starboard side. At nights a tent was rigged up on deck for sleeping quarters. The longship was sound and serviceable. She was an excellent craft to sail in. Yet most of all she was a beautiful vessel with slender, elegant lines. If the Viking raids ever pale into insignificance against modern barbarity, or if the Viking colonists are ever regarded as unworthy intruders on the European stage, the Gokstad longship will still remain as a timeless symbol of the craftsman's art and the sailor's daring.

This sturdily built ship unearthed at Gokstad would have been used by the Vikings for their swift and unexpected raids. *(University Museum of National Antiquities, Oslo, Norway)*

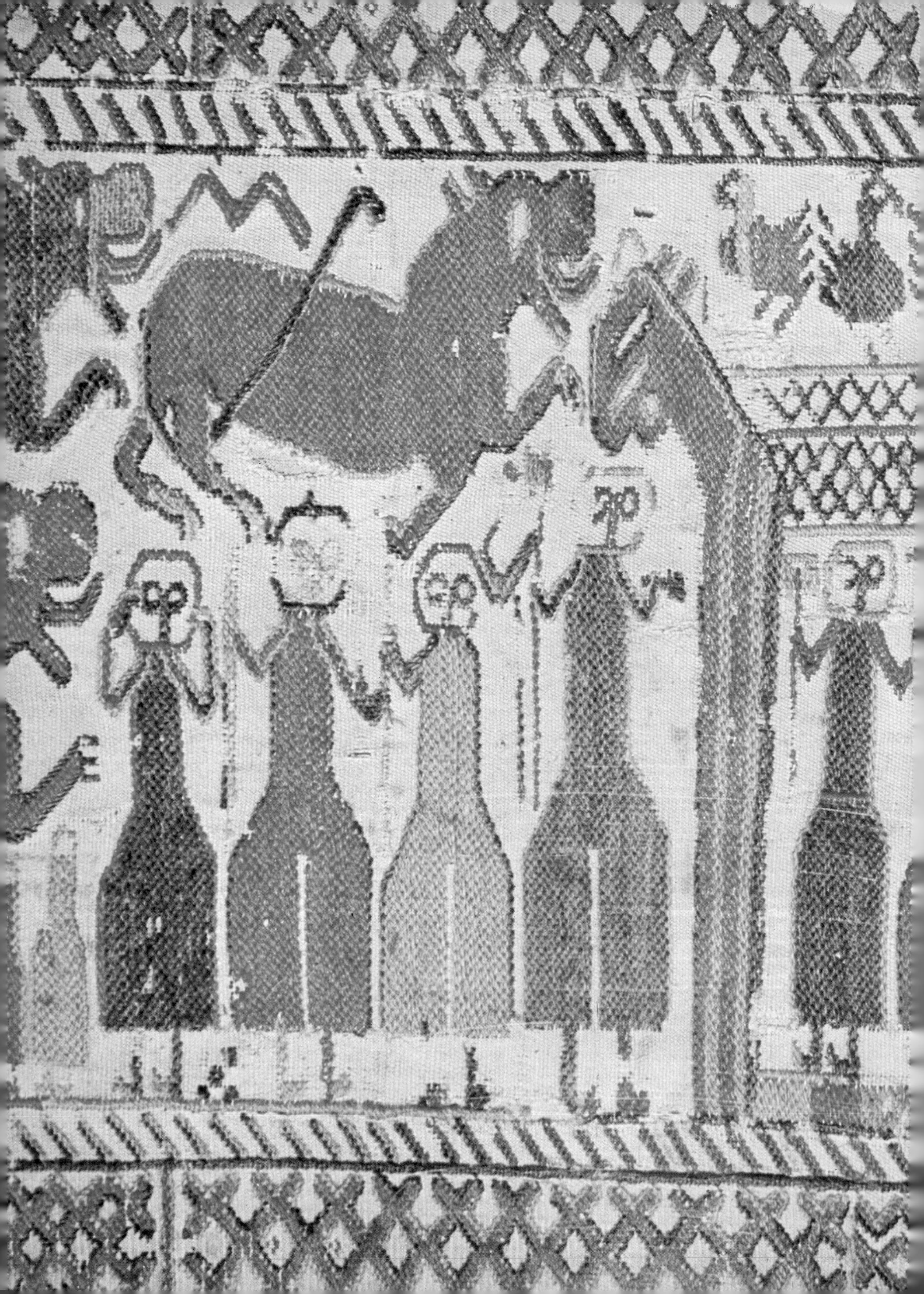